G000131242

LEARN TO PROGRAM YOUR
RASPBERRY PI

A hands-on guide to coding for beginners:
become a programmer, create games,
build a weather station and make a robot.

Kevin Partner

Published by Scribbleit.

Scribbleit Ltd, Long View, Alton, United Kingdom

This edition first published in February 2015

ISBN: 978-0-9574516-5-0

Copyright

Copyright © 2015 Kevin Partner. All rights reserved.

The right of the author to be identified as the author of this work has been asserted in accordance with the Copyright, Designs and Patents Act 1988. All rights reserved. No part of this publication may be reproduced, stored in a retrieval system, or transmitted, in any form or by any means, electronic, mechanical, photocopying, recording or otherwise, except as permitted by the UK Copyright, Designs and Patents Act 1988, without the prior permission of the publisher.

Disclaimer

Please note that this publication is intended as **general guidance only** and does not constitute professional advice. The author and Scribbleit Ltd make no representations or warranties with respect to the accuracy of completeness of the contents of this publication and cannot accept any responsibility for any liability, loss or risk, personal or otherwise which may arise, directly or indirectly, from reliance on information contained in this publication.

About the Author

Kevin Partner is a programmer, writer and unashamed geek. He's developed commercial applications and games in around a dozen languages, with Python as his current favourite. Kevin owns more Raspberry Pis than he'd care to admit to his wife and sees the Pi as the most revolutionary new computing device for many years.

Kevin, along with his long suffering wife Peta, also runs online craft retailer www.makingyourowncandles.co.uk. He wrote the best selling book "Your Craft Business: A Step by Step Guide" which has inspired hundreds of crafters to start their own businesses. Find out more here: http://scrib.me/craft_book

You can find out more about Kevin and see his other publications at **http://scrib.me/kev_p**

FREE Bonus Materials

Sign up to our list to get updates on the world of Raspberry Pi *and* **access to a bonus chapter on *How to create a security camera with your Raspberry Pi*** which makes for a perfect extra project once you've got to grips with basic Python programming.

Sign up here: ***http://scrib.me/rpisignup***

…you can unsubscribe at any time.

To Peta

How to use this book

This book contains **lots** of code samples and, to get the most out of it, I'd like to encourage you to type them in as we go along - just like in the pioneer days of the home computing boom when our idea of "entertainment" was to type pages of arcane code into our ZX Spectrums or BBC Micros. By doing this, us oldies learned how to program more or less by osmosis, it sort of sunk into our skin through our fingers. In this book, I cover a lot of ground very quickly as I believe strongly that you need to get into typing code quickly with only the minimum of preparation. I suggest you make sure you understand each new concept before progressing. If you get stuck, you can always email me at kevin.partner@scribbleit.co.uk.

Alongside this book, you'll also need a computer of some sort. For the early chapters and the two games, you can use a standard desktop PC or laptop to follow along but I hope, if you haven't already, that you'll take the plunge and invest in a Raspberry Pi - you won't regret it. Aside from within this book, you can access the accompanying code in two ways:

1) Download

You can download complete code from each of the main chapters to your computer, extract it and follow along. The links are given in the chapters themselves.

2) Shortcode

At various places, you'll see a short URL which you can type in so that you can view the code in a browser and, if you wish, copy/paste it.

Please make the effort to view the code samples in one of these two ways - there is little point in continuing if you're not prepared to do so as it will make little sense without the examples to hand.

Support

All the code, along with extra resources, can be found at the website I've created for this book: ***www.rpilab.net***

There's also a Facebook page at ***www.facebook.com/rpilab***

...but a better choice would be to follow the Google+ page at ***www.google.com/+RpilabNet***

You can also follow me on Twitter at ***@kevpartner***

Don't forget to sign up for a free extra project at ***http://scrib.me/rpisignup***

Contents

Build a robot   195

Part 1

Introducing the Raspberry Pi

The Raspberry Pi story

Raspberry Pi

Back in 2006, the Computer Laboratory at the University of Cambridge had a problem. Fewer and fewer students wanted to study Computer Science at the university, and the skill levels of those that did apply were declining year on year. Whereas, in the past, undergraduates already had coding experience – by the mid noughties, most knew much more about PowerPoint than programming.

This was partly due to a switch in emphasis at school towards teaching office applications and web design rather than how to program but it was also because the earlier generation of home computers had been replaced by games consoles. Why did that matter? Because a ZX Spectrum, BBC Model B micro or Commodore Amiga could be used both to play games and create software whereas the PS3 and Xbox, for all their technological superiority, are sealed units with no way for the average user to create their own games.

Perhaps the biggest problem, however, is caused by the way in which the internet has become part of everyday life. The average household now has at least one computer, usually a laptop, which they use for everything from banking, through online shopping to social networking and playing games. However, the idea of handing over this now critical piece of kit to an inexperienced student of programming fills the rest of the family with fear – what if their experiments led to a problem with their internet banking or, worse,

Facebook? There's another problem with modern laptops – they're simply over-the-top for learning to programme on. Over-powered, distracting and complicated, they're a million miles away from the blinking cursor of the classic home computers.

So, led by then Director of Studies Eben Upton, the group that would one day become the Raspberry Pi Foundation set themselves the target of encouraging 1,000 new computer science students across the UK. Since they couldn't directly re-write the syllabus taught in schools they decided to focus on what they could do – so they began work on an easy to program computer that would be, critically, cheap.

Fast forward to February 2012 and, after a 6 year journey, component suppliers Farnell and RS Electronics opened their websites for pre-orders of the Raspberry Pi. Having started the process with the aim of creating 1,000 per year, initial interest had been such that 10,000 were planned for production in 2012. Within minutes of going live with their Raspberry Pi order pages, both websites had collapsed and the initial allocation had disappeared in a wisp of smoke. A few days later and 100,000 pre-orders had been taken with around 4 million units estimated to have shipped by the end of 2014.

The original Raspberry Pi was labelled the Model B and this was followed by the Model A a few months later. In 2014, the Raspberry Pi Foundation released the B+ and A+ which featured better layouts for their respective purposes. In February 2015, the latest model, the Raspberry Pi V2 Model B, was released. This version features a much faster, more modern, processor and 1GB RAM so, for most purposes you'll want the V2 Model B. The A+ is ideal for purposes where low power consumption is critical (such as robotics) as it has only one USB port and no ethernet. Throughout this book, when I talk about the Raspberry Pi, you can assume I'm referring to the Version 2 Model B unless I specify otherwise.

Having said all that, if you have an existing Model A, Model B, Model A+ or Model B+ you will be able to follow every step of this book - you're losing nothing but a little speed when compared with the V2. This is a book about programming and all Raspberry Pi models are designed for that purpose.

The perfect platform for learning programming

The R-Pi has been designed from the ground up to provide the ideal environment for learning programming – whether that's simply for the fun of it or as the start of a career in coding. It's cheap, compact and rugged, and it also comes with most of the tools you need to create your own programs built into its default software. It may not be as fast as the family laptop but think about this – the computer controlling the Mars Curiosity rover currently trundling across the surface of the red planet is less powerful than a £30 Raspberry Pi. If NASA's chip can power a space probe, just imagine what you can do with your Pi.

What is the Raspberry Pi?

The first thing you'll notice when you first clap eyes on a Raspberry Pi B+ is that it's tiny – the size of a credit card. Then you'll notice that it has no case – it's simply a printed circuit board. Despite its diminutive size and Heath Robinson appearance, however, the R-Pi is a completely functional computer. And it costs around £30.

Let's take a look at what makes it tick.

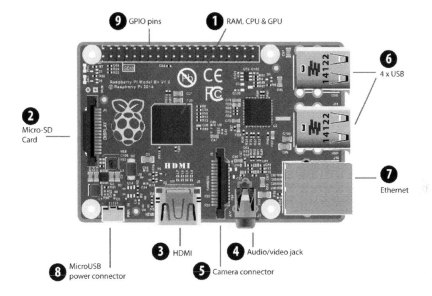

9 GPIO pins
1 RAM, CPU & GPU
6 4 x USB
2 Micro-SD Card
7 Ethernet
3 HDMI
4 Audio/video jack
8 MicroUSB power connector
5 Camera connector

Brains

With the B+, a single chip (1) contains memory, the central processing unit and graphics chip whereas the Version 2 Pi has the memory underneath the circuit board.

CPU

The Raspberry Pi uses a mobile phone chip made by ARM - the company that makes the CPUs used in the vast majority of smartphones and tablets, including those sold by Apple. To keep costs down, the version used in the R-Pi is slower than you'd find in an iPad, for example, but it's fast enough to do the job it's intended for.

GPU

In contrast with the relatively pedestrian CPU, the Graphics Processing Unit on the R-Pi is equivalent to a modern smartphone or tablet. This means it can run many 3D games as well as being perfect as a very cheap media centre computer (indeed, this is one of the most common uses for the R-Pi). Load up the right software, connect it to your TV and broadband and you have iPlayer, YouTube and other internet broadcasting services at your fingertips.

Memory

The Model B+ comes with 512MB of Random Access Memory (RAM), the Version 2 Raspberry Pi has a massive 1GB – plenty for the uses we're going to put it to. It also comes with an MicroSD card slot (2) – exactly the same as that used by many smartphones – which takes the place of the hard disk found in most laptops. Programs are stored on the MicroSD card and, once the Pi is powered on, these are copied into the much faster RAM until the computer is turned off, when the RAM is cleared. One of the great advantages of the Pi is that you can turn it from a media player to a desktop computer simply by swapping out the MicroSD card – much easier than removing a laptop's hard disk!

Note - the original Model B and Model A used standard SD cards rather than MicroSD. They work identically.

Sound and Vision

One of the design requirements for the Raspberry Pi was that it should be easy to hook up to your existing equipment, so it includes an HDMI port (3) so you can connect it to your TV or a spare computer monitor. Bear in mind that HDMI carries both picture and sound so if you use a monitor, you may need to plug a set of speakers into the Audio/Video jack (4).

If your monitor doesn't have an HDMI socket, you can buy a cheap adaptor to convert it to DVI or VGA.

If you're really stuck, you can use the Audio/Video jack (4) to connect to an old-fashioned CRT TV. However, this was added mainly to allow the R-Pi to be used in the third world where TVs are more common than monitors – the picture quality is poor.

Connections

The Raspberry Pi Model B+ and Version 2 come with four USB ports (6) which you can use to connect a keyboard, mouse, wifi dongle or any compatible peripheral. You may want to buy a USB hub to allow you to plug in more devices at once.

You can connect the Raspberry Pi directly to your router or a wired network via the standard Ethernet port (7) – this gives the fastest and most reliable connection to the Internet.

Pi Pins

So far, everything we've described (apart from the MicroSD Card) is pretty standard to all computers. However, the Pi has some extra capabilities not found on your common or garden laptop. The most important of these are the General Purpose Input Output (GPIO) pins (9) – these offer various ways to control devices and receive input from sensors and such like. However, misusing these pins can bake your Pi so it's best to use one of the many add-on boards that allow you to experiment safely. We cover some of the options later.

The Pi also includes a connector for a camera module and a DSI connector that can be used to connect the Pi to certain specialist displays such as mobile phone screens.

So this is a small, cheap computer with no moving parts and the ability to connect with the outside world. Put another way, imagine having the power of a laptop without its bulk or its fragility. With a Raspberry Pi you can take computing almost anywhere – think about the possibilities.

- You can hook it up to a webcam, attach it to a weather balloon , get permission, launch and take pictures from near space. http://www.raspberrypi.org/archives/1620 (the Raspberry Pi survived falling 40km through the atmosphere when the balloon burst)

- Attach temperature, humidity and air pressure sensors to create an intelligent weather station

- Create a media centre for the car or home

- Build it into a bird box, along with infra-red trip sensors and a web cam, to record the nesting season: www.youtube.com/watch?V=JpbFBCndo

- Put together a very cheap internet radio

- Use it as the brains of a robot

...as well as a general purpose (if a little slow) computer. For less than £30!

And that's just the beginning.

Where can I Get One?

Farnell: http://scrib.me/farnell_rpi

RS Electronics: http://scrib.me/rs_rpi

The Raspberry Pi Foundation selected Premier Farnell and RS Electronics to be their official suppliers so we recommend buying direct from them. Whilst they're also available on ebay, Amazon and through some retailers, you're likely to get the lowest price and the latest models by going direct. As an example, in September 2012, the foundation launched a slightly revised version of the Pi that included double the memory of the original model – customers of Farnell and RS Electronics automatically received the new version on launch.

If you don't have a MicroSD card already then you may want to add one to your order when you buy your Pi – that way you'll know it's compatible (although the vast majority of bog standard cards work fine). Either way an 8GB card is about the right size. I don't recommend that you buy one with the operating system (OS) already installed. This is because the Raspberry Pi is designed to be a "hands on" computer and you'll learn a lot more by installing the OS yourself. Sooner or later you'll want to upgrade the OS so it makes sense to get to grips with the process right at the start. It isn't difficult and you'll also save yourself a few pounds.

Setting up your Raspberry Pi

Once the jiffy bag containing your tiny new computer lands on the mat you have a little work to do before you can connect it to a display and boot it up. The Raspberry Pi uses a standard MicroSD card instead of the hard disk you'd find in most laptops and your first job is to install the software needed to run the computer onto the MicroSD card. It's not difficult, just follow the steps.

FOCUS ON: RASPBIAN

There wouldn't be a lot of point in a £30 computer if you were then required to install an expensive operating system on it (such as Windows or Apple's OSX) to get it to work. This means that the various OSes so far created for it are all based on the free and open-source Linux. The specific variety recommended by the foundation is called Raspbian, a version of Debian which is a widespread and very popular distribution of Linux. If this all sounds like so much gobbledygook, don't worry – if you've used Windows, you'll find Raspbian pretty familiar. You can even install Linux versions of many of the programs you're familiar with including LibreOffice for Microsoft-compatible word processing and spreadsheet work, and even the Chrome browser – we'll cover how to do this shortly. In fact, you'd be hard pressed to find any computing activity for which mature and competent software doesn't exist for Raspbian.

Microsoft has announced that it's developing a version of the forthcoming Windows 10 that will work on the Raspberry Pi Version 2. Whilst this is very good news, Raspbian will remain the better choice for programmers and hobbyists as it has Python built in and amazing community support.

Stage 1: Prepare your MicroSD Card

You need a Windows-based computer for this. If your PC has an MicroSD card slot, then go right ahead and insert your 8GB+ card. If not, you'll need to use an adaptor. **Red Alert**: if you use an external hard drive then disconnect it now so there's no risk of accidentally picking the wrong drive letter when you reformat the MicroSD card.

The simplest way to get up an running is to use the "NOOBS" software provided by the Raspberry Pi Foundation. Go to www.raspberrypi.org/downloads/ (scrib.me/rpi_noobs) and click the *Download ZIP* button beneath the heading NOOBS (*NOT* NOOBS LITE). This will download an archive containing the files needed to the downloads folder on your PC.

Once the ZIP has downloaded, go to the folder on your PC in Windows Explorer and find it. Right click the file and select *Extract All* and then *Extract*. This creates a subfolder containing the files. Open this folder and then select all its files and subfolders (the easiest way to do this is to click on one of the files - *bootcode.bin* for example - then press CTRL-A) and drag them all onto the drive containing your MicroSD card.

Stage 2: Hook up your Raspberry Pi

Connect the HDMI lead to your TV or monitor (hint: if your monitor doesn't have HDMI but does have DVI, you can get a cheap adaptor). Now, connect the keyboard and mouse to the USB ports and the ethernet port to your internet router or network. If you don't plan to use the Raspberry Pi near your router you can use a compatible wifi dongle (a good example being the Edimax EW-7811UN)

Now connect the power. After a few seconds, a graphical box will appear with a list of operating systems you can choose. Click the check box next to *Raspbian* and then click the *Install* button just above. The other OSes on that list are alternatives you might want to consider for another MicroSD card (remember, you can turn your Raspberry Pi into a completely new computer by simply swapping cards) - for example, two of the OSes are specifically designed for creating a media centre.

You can now sit back and wait for Raspbian to be installed - it'll take a few minutes. Click OK when it's finished and the Pi will reboot.

When you first boot up, the Pi will present a configuration screen with various options – you can move up and down the list using the arrow keys, along with enter and escape.

Choose item 3 (Enable Boot) and select the second option *Desktop Log in as user 'pi' at the graphical desktop* so that the Windows style graphical user interface loads by default.

- I suggest also choosing option 5 *Enable Camera* if you intend to follow all the exercises in this book.

- Now select option 7 *Overclock* and select *Modest* to get a slight performance boost without risking the processor unnecessarily.

- Now choose option 8 *Advanced Options*. If you have more than one Pi, you might want to give this one its own Hostname (option A2).

- You should enable SSH (*A4*) as this will allow you to log into your Pi from another computer when you want to run it without a monitor, keyboard and mouse. At some point in the future, depending on which projects you work on, you might also want to enable SPI and I2C but, for now, once you've enabled SSH, you can go back to the main menu.

Use the arrow keys to move down the menu, then across to *Finish* and press Enter, then *Yes* to Reboot.

All being well, your Raspberry Pi will reboot into a desktop view that, on the surface at least, is pretty familiar.

Top-left you'll see the equivalent of Windows 7's Start button which gives access to the software that comes pre-installed on the Raspberry Pi. Next to the Start button is an icon that launches the built-in browser and next to this the *File Manager* – which works in a similar way to the Windows File Explorer.

The next icon along launches *LXTerminal* which is a window containing the text "pi@raspberrypi" in green at the top left. We'll use this window to type various commands – don't worry, you'll only ever need to learn a few.

FOCUS ON: WIRELESS

As a general rule, Linux distributions have poorer support for wireless networking than Windows PCs or Macs because not all manufacturers write drivers for their products. This also applies to wireless keyboards and mice, so you must make sure that a device is compatible with your Raspberry Pi before purchasing. You can find a list of supported devices at *http://scrib.me/rpi_verified*. The Edimax EW-7811UN wifi dongle is a good choice for most situations because, as well as being compatible, it also performs well despite its diminutive size.

To install, plug the dongle into the Raspberry Pi before switching it on. Once booted up, click the *Menu* button, choose *Preferences* and click the *Wi-fi Configuration* option. Choose the *Manage Networks* tab, then the *Scan* button. You'll see a list of local wifi networks. Double click yours and complete the network properties dialog box – remembering to enter your wireless password into the PSK field. Now click *Add* and you should find you're connected.

Stage 3: Find and install software

The Raspberry Pi comes with a basic range of software but one of the benefits of choosing a Linux-based system is that it gives you access to a huge library of free programmes. We're going to begin by installing an easy to use editor for our coding.

Finding and installing software for the Raspberry Pi is one activity that's very different to its Windows equivalent. Rather than running a setup programme, with Linux you use a "package manager" and, in many cases this is done by typing in commands – don't panic it's easy! We're going to cover how to do it via the terminal first because most online examples use this approach.

Each distribution of Linux comes with its own library of optional software – these are called Package Repositories. It would be wasteful to install the entire library when you set up a new computer so you should think of the initial setup as a starting point – you then add software from the repositories to suit the purpose you have in mind. For a general purpose computer, you'd probably want to install an office suite such as LibreOffice (a version of OpenOffice) but we're going to focus mainly on installing a programming editor and, at various points throughout the book, we'll add extra packages.

Let's begin by installing Geany which is the programming editor I recommend. Double click *LXTerminal* and type the following:

sudo apt-get update

...followed by the enter key. This probably looks incomprehensible so let's take it step by step. The first command, *sudo*, tells Linux that you want to run the rest of the commands as a "super-user". This is similar to the Administrator user in Windows – it gives permission to change the system which means it can be dangerous if not used properly. So, at the start of a line that is going to install programs, for example, we have to explicitly type sudo to give our account permission to do so.

"apt" is short for "Advanced Packaging Tool" and this is the set of tools we're going to run to install our software.

"get" is the utility within apt that does this – it gets packages.

Finally *"update"* tells apt-get to download the latest list of packages – you should always update apt-get before trying to install software.

Now, to actually install Geany we can type:

sudo apt-get install geany

...and enter. The first two chunks are the same but this time we tell *apt-get* to "install" a package and then the name of the package itself. Your terminal window will now fill up with lines of text explaining what it's doing – you can go and make a cup of tea as the whole thing takes place automatically. Once done, Geany will be available from the *Programming* submenu of the Start button. If you want an icon on the desktop, right click the icon in the submenu and select *Add to desktop*.

This is all very well, but how do you know what to install and what the package name is? One way is to google "office software for

Raspberry Pi", for example, but another is to install a graphical package manager. Type:

sudo apt-get install synaptic

This will download and install the Synaptic Package Manager. Once this is done, you will find it by clicking the *Start* button and choosing the *Preferences* submenu. Click *Synaptic* and you'll be asked to type your password (which, unless you've changed it, will be "raspberry"). You'll now see a window containing all the packages available to the Raspberry Pi, organised by type.

We're going to use Synaptic to install a game. On the left side of the Synaptic window, scroll down to the *Games and Amusement* category. Now scroll through the right hand window until you find *Gweled*, then select *Mark for Installation*. Once you've done this, click the *Apply* button to install it.

That was straightforward but it's worth remembering that the equivalent command in the terminal would have been...

sudo apt-get install gweled

...which is clearly much quicker. So, if you know the package name, you should use the command line approach, if you want to browse, choose Synaptic. For now, why not have a go at Gweled which is a Bejeweled clone - you'll see the point of this later in the book.

The Flip Side

You now have a fully working Pi, ready and raring to go but, as you think about all the possibilities that are now opening up before you, bear in mind the following:

The Pi is Slow. If you're used to the snappiness of a modern computer, using heavyweight software such as LibreOffice on the A, B, A+ or B+ models will feel like wading through treacle. You'll notice a delay of a couple of seconds after you double click an icon before anything seems to happen, for example. This is partly to do with the fact that a MicroSD Card is not as fast as a modern hard disk when it comes to reading large numbers of small files, rather than the lack of speed of the processor. Once your word processor has fully loaded, you'll probably find the performance perfectly acceptable.

Some games will work well on the Pi – 3D shoot-em-up Quake was famously ported across very early on. However, the Pi is not designed as a gaming device for playing high-end games so don't imagine it'll replace an Xbox for that purpose.

Linux is not Windows/OSX. Although the Raspberry Pi desktop looks superficially similar to Windows, underneath the surface there are many differences. Just about anything you could accomplish in Windows or OSX, you can achieve just as well in Raspbian – but allow yourself extra time for research.

Not all hardware will work. Partly because the Pi runs a variety of Linux and partly because it uses an ARM chip, some keyboards, mice, printers, wifi dongles and other peripherals will not work. You should always check the list of approved hardware or, if buying online, check the reviews to see if others state the product works with the Raspberry Pi. Rest assured, however, that most standard hardware works fine.

Having said all that, most people will consider these limitations a small price to pay for a tiny, portable, durable computer costing around £30 that can open up a huge range of creative possibilities.

Part 2

GETTING SET UP FOR PROGRAMMING

What is programming?

Mention the word "programming" to most people and one of two images will pop into their minds – the t-shirted hacker wreaking havoc with sensitive government servers, or lines of incomprehensible code streaming down a screen. Not surprisingly, real programming is nothing like either.

Wikipedia defines it as "the process of designing, writing, testing, debugging, and maintaining the source code of computer programs" which is a bit like saying that running is something you do when you run. Of course, programming means to write code – but what is that code for? What is the point?

The fact is that inside every single electronic device lurks code that was written by a programmer. It's no exaggeration to say that programming makes the modern world go round. By learning how to code, then, you are able to take an active part in shaping the environment you and others live in. While that might sound a little grand or abstract, just remember that a person, or a team of people, created the code that runs the microwave you use to make cheesy beans for supper, the fuel injection system that gets you from A to B and the set-top box you use to watch your time shifted TV programmes, as well as the more obvious code you encounter on your computer, games console or smartphone.

Someone must write the instructions that make these devices carry out their useful functions and, despite what you might imagine, it's not rocket science. Above all else, programming involves two main skills – creative imagination and the ability to think in a logical, structured way. It certainly doesn't involve remembering every obscure command of every coding language – that's Google's job. Programming is a process in the same sense as planning a presentation, cooking a complex meal or coming up with next season's Football Manager strategy. It's like solving a puzzle and it's one of the most enjoyable and creative things you'll ever do.

Don't believe me? Just have a little patience and you'll soon enough discover the thrill of taking control of your computer rather than feeling a slave to it. This is at the heart of programming – having an impact in the real world whether that's on a PC screen, smartphone or a hacked-together robot trundling after the dog. This impact can be profound and when the penny drops, you'll realise that programming frees you from being a passenger in this technological world and provides the toolkit to take the wheel for yourself.

Setting your sights

With such a wealth of possibilities it's important to think about what you want to achieve with your programming skills. Having a practical use in mind will help make sense of what you're learning as well as giving you a chance to practice and get a sense of real achievement. The best advice is to follow your interests and choose a project you'll enjoy. Whether or not you want to become a professional programmer, by focusing on something that you'll enjoy for its own sake, you'll become better quicker. The people at the top of the industry, earning fat paycheques creating the software than runs the banks and businesses almost always began this way, and many code for fun in their spare time.

So what is achievable for a keen beginner willing to invest some time, effort and brainpower to learn programming skills?

Making Games

Most coders begin by creating games because most like playing games so they start off with an understanding of how they work (whether they realise this or not) which means, crucially, they know what they're aiming for when they're developing their game.

The games category covers everything from basic word guessing puzzles, through 2D platform adventures to immersive first-person extravaganzas such as the Call of Duty series. As a new programmer, you'll begin at the simple end before settling on your favourite form – many people choose arcade puzzlers or point-and-click adventures, for example, because these can be created in small teams or even by coders working alone. Whatever your ultimate ambition, games are a great way to learn programming.

Mobile Apps

The market for smartphone and tablet apps has become hugely popular in the past few years - especially amongst "indie" developers (that's you). One reason for this is that mobile represents the fastest growing category of internet connected hardware. Even more importantly, each main platform (iOS, Android and Windows) is controlled by marketplaces that make it easy for individual developers to publish their work. You don't need to sign a deal with a major distributor such as EA Games to get your masterpiece into the pockets and hands of your audience – you create it and publish it direct, at minimal cost.

That's not to say it's all plain sailing – despite what you might hear, mobile app development is no gravy train. But it is the leading modern platform and a good sector to learn if you're looking for a career in programming.

Web Development

By creating applications that run on a web server, you potentially get all the benefits of developing apps for mobile devices as well as having your software available to the billions of users of standard PCs. Whilst there are many situations where an app is a better choice (games being one), it's often most effective to put the code on the web and have people access it via a browser.

Much of this programming goes unnoticed – but it's there lurking in the background every time you order something from Amazon or post a status update on Facebook. Anything that happens on the web beyond serving up static web pages is programming. To see an example of just how stunning this can be, take a look at http://www.movikantirevo.com/

PC Applications

There's still a big market for software that users download and run on their computer. This can include utilities, games, educational software and creative programs such as music editors and art packages. In practice, this usually means that you spot a problem that needs solving and, if you can't find a good pre-existing solution to it, you write your own program. You'd be amazed at the tiny niches some of this software fulfils – there are, for example, several "explosion generator" applications that satisfy the need for arcade game developers to blow up enemy spaceships in spectacular style.

Typically, the coder creates a solution to their own problem and then, if they think there would be an audience for it, spends time adding an effective user interface (windows, dialog boxes and buttons) before releasing it for general use. It's also common to contribute the code to the open-source community which means that anyone could amend it. Done in an organised way, this can result in a much better, more widely used, program – for which you get the main credit. Very good for your CV!

Controlling your home

With the Raspberry Pi and related technologies such as the Arduino (www.arduino.cc), it's become much simpler to program real world objects as well as traditional computers. There's nothing quite as cool as connecting with your environment, whether that's keeping tabs on your energy bills, watching a robot you've made from an old remote control toy make its way around the living room floor or taking pictures from a weather balloon. The range of possibilities is infinite and it's in this area that the Raspberry Pi has a big advantage over a laptop, say – its diminutive size, modest power requirements, robustness and, above all, low cost make it ideal for real world projects.

...and that's just the beginning. As you develop your programming skills, you'll notice more and more opportunities to put them to work – now it's time to tool up and get cracking.

What do you need?

So you want to be a coder – but what hardware and software do you need to get started? The good news is that the hardware is cheap and the software is free. By using a version of Linux as the operating system, you can learn to code on a low cost computer such as the Raspberry Pi or a re-purposed laptop or desktop that's now too slow to run Windows. Popular Linux variants such as Raspbian, Debian and Ubuntu are free, as is most of the software you can run on them – including many of the most popular programming languages.

Parlez-vous Python?

The first choice you need to make is which programming language to learn – and there are hundreds to choose from. The best choice would be one that's widely used, easy to learn, applicable to lots of programming tasks and similar enough to other languages to make it easy to spread your wings later. It should also be free. At http://scrib.me/tiobeRPI you'll find a table of languages in order of their popularity in terms of jobs and online resources. The only candidate that meets all our criteria is Python. Here's why:

Widely Used: Python appears in the top ten of the TIOBE index (at the time of writing) which means that many skilled engineers use it, and there are plenty of resources to help learn it (including this book) as well as jobs for Python programmers

Easy to learn: The Raspberry Pi Foundation chose Python as its recommended programming language for this reason. One way to describe a language is to say how "high level" it is – broadly speaking, the more English-like it looks, the more high level it's considered. Take a look at the following code – it shows how to simply make the words "Hello World!" appear on screen. The first example is from C, a very widely used but low level language. The second is Python.

HELLO WORLD

```
HELLO WORLD - in C
#include <stdio.h>
int main(int argc, char *argv[])
{
    printf("Hello world!\N");
    return 0;
}
HELLO WORLD  - in Python
print "Hello World!"
```

Not only is the Python example much closer to English, and therefore easier to understand, it's also much shorter – another feature of high level languages.

Flexible: You've probably heard of BASIC which is another easy to learn, widely used language. However, Visual Basic is the only dialect that appears in the top twenty and it is restricted to Windows computers – the commercial version is also relatively expensive. Python, on the other hand, can be used on Windows, Mac and Linux computers as well as on many other platforms. It's also able to access libraries of code created in C and C++.

A good first language: Python is similar to many of the other popular languages. Once you've learned to code in Python, then, you'll find it much easier to get to grips with almost any other main-stream language.

...and if you need any other reason – it's named for Monty Python!

FOCUS ON: PYTHON SQUARED

There are two families of Python in common use – 2.x and 3.x. This probably seems odd as it's usually the case that when a new version of any software comes out (Python 3 was released in 2008) users tend to upgrade. However, one of Python's great strengths is the huge library of add-ons created by the Python community and some of these are written in version 2, making them incompatible with the latest version.

The differences between versions 2 and 3 are minimal so, in this book, we're focusing on Python 2.7 – the version that comes installed by default in Raspbian at the time of writing this book. This means we can use just about every available Python library but still move interchangeably between it and version 3 when the time comes.

Tools of the trade

The good news is that you probably already have the hardware you need to become a programmer – and if you don't, it needn't be at all expensive. Whilst Python is available for all the main operating systems, its natural home is Linux. One advantage of this is that distributions such as Debian will run on low-specification computers (which is why it was chosen - in its Raspbian form - for the Raspberry Pi), meaning you can breathe new life into that old laptop in the loft.

If you already have a laptop running a recent Windows version or Mac OSX, you can add Linux to it alongside your existing operating system – we'll cover how to do that shortly. Ideally, however, you should have a dedicated computer – however old. All you need to supply is a monitor or TV, keyboard and mouse – and you're off!

Even if you own a Raspberry Pi, you might want to develop on another, more powerful computer and then move the code across to the Pi. This is very useful if you set up your RPi in your living room, shed or, indeed, robot as it's very easy to connect to the Pi across a network.

Ubuntu

If you're using a Raspberry Pi, you should already be set up with Raspbian. What if you want to stick with your existing PC? You can install Python for Windows but we recommend using Linux as the basis of your programming environment. Why? Well, it's Python's natural environment and if you intend to do any serious coding you'll almost certainly encounter Linux at some point – especially if you develop for the internet. Finally, Linux is made for tinkering – it's a much more open OS than either Windows or OSX and has an active community providing all the bits and pieces you need to create great programs, as well as generous and enthusiastic advice.

For most people, Ubuntu is the best Linux distribution to choose. It's based on Debian (like Raspbian) but is more user friendly – it's the most widely used and most actively developed version of Linux. You can also install it in several ways, depending on your situation:

Wipeout: If you want to repurpose an old laptop then your best bet is probably to wipe whatever version of Windows is already on it and replace it with Ubuntu (having backed-up any documents you want to keep). To do this, go to http://www.ubuntu.com/download/desktop and download the newest version. The download is in the form of an ISO file which you can either burn to DVD (double click it and follow the prompts) or transfer to a USB Flash drive.

When you're ready to install it on the target computer, insert the DVD or Flash drive and follow the prompts – full instructions are on the Ubuntu downloads page.

Virtually Ubuntu: Perhaps the most flexible option is to have Ubuntu as a "virtual machine" (VM) running in Windows. A VM is a software program that pretends it's a hardware computer running your chosen operating system (Ubuntu in this case). The great benefit of this approach is that if something goes wrong, you can very quickly wipe it and start again. To create a VM, you need software such as Oracle's VirtualBox (https://www.virtualbox.org/wiki/Downloads). Once installed, you can set up a VM and then load the Ubuntu .iso file into it – in fact you can create as many VMs as you have space, allowing you to try out any number of different versions of Linux.

FOCUS ON: PYTHON ON WINDOWS

Windows is the only major operating system that doesn't come with Python built in. If, for whatever reason, you're forced to work in Windows, you should download the Windows installer at http://www.python.org/getit/ - choose the latest version of Python 2.

The Programmer's Toolkit

You need three things for most coding tasks: a programming language, an editor and media packages for creating the images, sounds and other resources your project uses.

Language

The Raspberry Pi comes with Python 2.7 built-in – this is the latest, and final, version of the Python 2 family and the code examples in this book are aimed at 2.7. We'll cover how to make sure you're targeting the right version in a moment.

Editor

Computer programs are, usually, text files so you can edit them using any word processor or text editor. However, by using an IDE (Integrated Development Environment) rather than, for example, Leafpad (the Raspberry Pi's equivalent of Windows Notepad) you get access to all sorts of tools that help with your programming.

Raspbian includes two versions of an editor called IDLE – one for Python 2.7 and one for Python 3 – but it's rather too basic for convenient programming and so the examples in this book have been created using Geany. If you followed the walkthrough in part 1 to set up your Raspberry Pi, then you've probably already installed Geany – if not, simply open up LX Terminal and type:

> *sudo apt-get update*

> *sudo apt-get install geany*

...pressing *Enter* after each. The first line ensures the list of packages on your Raspberry Pi is up to date, the second line performs the actual install.

If you're using Windows, go to www.geany.org/Download/Releases and select the latest version of the Full Installer.

Geany

1: Toolbar

The Geany toolbar contains shortcuts for moving quickly through your code, picking and inserting colours and running your program with a single click

2: Code Explorer

The left hand pane displays information about the program you're currently working on – including easy access to its main parts.

3: Coding Window

This is where you'll be spending most of your time. Geany includes:

- *Code suggestion*: it guesses what you're typing and offers to finish for you

- *In-built reference*: when you type the name of a Python statement, it shows what that function expects to follow it and how it works

- *Syntax colouring*: "syntax" means that words and numbers that make up your code. By automatically applying different colours to different types of syntax, Geany makes your code much easier to read and debug.

4: Message Window
Geany displays messages and status reports in this window – you can also select the Terminal tab to get quick access to the LXTerminal.

Media
Many projects require custom graphics and, for games, you'll probably need to create or edit your own sound effects. As with text editors, there are many choices available to Linux users but the gloriously named "GNU Image Manipulation Program" - GIMP to its adherents – is the most fully featured and best supported. For sound editing, the best choice is Audacity.

GIMP
To install GIMP on your Raspberry Pi start up Synaptic Package Manager and find gimp in the Graphics category. Select this and also gimp-data then click Apply. Alternatively, from LXTerminal, enter the following line

> *sudo apt-get update*

> *sudo apt-get install gimp*

Once installed, you'll find an icon to run GIMP in the Graphics folder of your start menu. GIMP is a processor-intensive application so it'll run fairly slowly on your Raspberry Pi but it's perfectly usable. However, to get the best possible speed. it's worth shutting down any other applications before running it.

Windows users can download a GIMP installer from http://gimp-win.sourceforge.net/stable.html

Whichever OS you're using, you'll find GIMP reasonably familiar if you've used any other photo editing package, whether that's Windows Paint or Photoshop. You can find out more about GIMP at http://www.gimp.org/

Audacity

Most games include sound effects and even if you use pre-existing resources, the chances are you'll need to edit them to fit your project sooner or later. Audacity is a basic sound editing package that includes all the functionality you're likely to need. In Synaptic, you'll find Audacity in the Multimedia category – again you need to make sure that both audacity and audacity-data are selected before you click Apply.

To install via LXTerminal:

> *sudo apt-get update*

> *sudo apt-get install audacity*

- bearing in mind that if you've only just installed GIMP, you don't need to run the update command again.

Once installed, you'll find Audacity in the Sound & Video section of your Start menu. You can find out more about Audacity, along with links to download it for Windows and Mac at http://audacity.sourceforge.net/

Let's Get Cracking

The final step before we get into coding is to check that your Python environment is working as expected. Rather than bashing out the bog standard, boring, "hello world" programme we're going to create a real-time clock for your desktop. This is not only more interesting and useful but also tests whether you have two of the most important Python libraries installed and working as well as Python itself.

1: Connect your Pi and load up the desktop. Open Geany by going to the Programming folder of the Start menu.

2: Click *File, New* and then immediately save it as "clock.py" - the "py" extension tells Geany that you're creating a Python file and switches on its built-in help and syntax colouring. Now, go to the *Edit* menu in Geany and click *Preferences*. Pick the *Editor* tab on the left followed by the *Display* tab along the top then click next to *"Show white space"* to fill in the checkbox. This means that all spaces and tabs are marked in the editor window – something that's very helpful when typing and editing Python code. Click *Apply*.

3: Type the code at this location into Geany:

```
1   import time,pygame
2   pygame.init()
3   theFont=pygame.font.Font(None,72)
4   clock = pygame.time.Clock()
5   screen = pygame.display.set_mode([320, 200])
6   pygame.display.set_caption('Pi Time')
7
8   while True:
9       clock.tick(1)
10      theTime=time.strftime("%H:%M:%S",time.localtime())
11      timeText=theFont.render(str(theTime),True,(255,255,255),(0,0,0))
12      screen.blit(timeText,(80,60))
13      pygame.display.update()
14
```

http://scrib.me/clock_rpi

Be particularly careful to use tabs to indent your code exactly as shown in the listing. Although it probably looks like gobbledygook at the moment, you can see immediately how little code is needed to create a real, working application. For now, we're just testing that your setup is working so, once you've typed it in, click the Cog icon on the Geany toolbar to run the app.

All being well, after a short pause, your clock will pop up and start ticking away. If so, congratulations – you've demonstrated that Geany, Python and the pygame module are working together. If the clock doesn't appear, take a look at the LXTerminal window as it'll contain a message that will help you diagnose the problem - it'll almost always be a mistake in typing the code.

Here's the clock working on a Raspberry Pi:

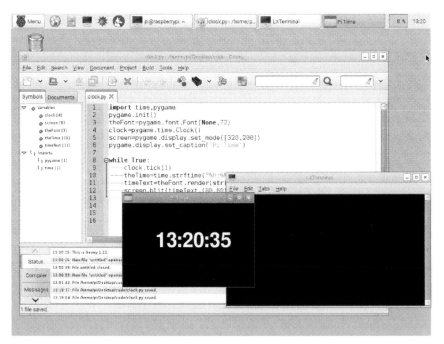

Once the clock is working, you're ready to get cracking – you now have everything you need to begin your career as a programmer. Let's go.

Programming – from the inside out

Computers, micro-controllers and other electronic devices are used for such a wide range of tasks that you might imagine they'd share very little in common. However, whether they're running on an Xbox, inside the dashboard of a car or controlling the Curiosity Rover on the surface of Mars, most programs work in a similar way – they take input, apply logic to it and then output the results. Some very simple programs do this once each time they're run – for example a calculator – but most applications go through this loop many times per second. As a programmer, then, almost everything you'll ever do will fall into one of these three categories and knowing how they work makes understanding how code is put together much simpler.

Let's look at a few examples to see how this works in practice.

A VAT Calculator (yawn!)

Yes, it's boring but somebody has to write programs to carry out useful, if mundane, tasks like this. A VAT calculator would ask the user to type in an amount, it would then work out the VAT on that amount and add it to arrive at a total. Finally the program would display the result on screen.

In this case, then, the amount entered by the user is the input, the VAT calculation is the logic and displaying the result on-screen is the output. Bear in mind that the output could just as easily be to a printer or even a speech synthesiser – however, if that was the case, neither of the first two parts would be affected. Whilst this might make little difference on a tiny app such as this, on large corporate systems splitting the code into these three purposes makes it possible for different programmers to work on each and for the application to be easily ported from desktop to web to mobile.

Forza Motorsport for Xbox

This is more like it! In a driving game, the player uses a controller or steering wheel as input and the console then translates the directional changes and applies them to its calculations of the car's position using its logic code. Once it has done this, it generates and displays the output in the form of graphics on the screen. Given the frame-rate of a modern console game, this is happening many times per second – not just for the visuals but also for the sound effects. In that case, the input might be the controller buttons assigned to acceleration and braking, the logic involves applying the correct physics to the Xbox's model of the game world and the output, along with the visual elements, includes the sound of a thrashed engine or screaming brakes.

Mars Rover

Right now, around 225 million miles away, a robot the size of a Ford Fiesta is wending its way across the surface of Mars. Controlling the Curiosity Mars rover is a computer less powerful than your Raspberry Pi. This computer, the RAD750 created by a subsidiary of British company BAE Systems, contains over 2 million lines of code written in C – although Python was used to create testing scripts.

This code controls everything from sensing the environment to navigating the rover through the Martian landscape. Because radio waves take over 12 minutes to travel between Mission Control and Mars, the rover cannot be driven like a remote control car. So it includes software that uses its cameras (input) to determine where rocks and other obstructions are, calculates a safe path (logic) and turns the wheels (output).

And bear in mind that human beings wrote the code – and they started programming with as little knowledge as you have right now.

Clock

Finally, remember the tiny clock app we created in the last section? It took the current system clock time as input, converted it to a human-readable form (logic) and displayed it on-screen (output).

A Simple Game

So most programs take input, process that information using logic and then output it in some form – we can use this information when we design and write our applications. For example, let's say you've decided to create an old-school arcade game. In your mind's eye you see different fruit falling from the top of the screen, some of them raspberries. The player uses a laser-gun that moves across the bottom of the screen attempting to shoot the raspberries but miss all the other fruit. Without some sort of model in mind, you'd struggle to work out where to begin and how to organise your thoughts. The ILO model gives you a template to help get started.

Input

We begin by thinking about what inputs the game will take from the user. During the game, the player needs a way of controlling the laser gun so we need to decide if that's going to be achieved by keyboard, mouse or touch. The choice depends largely on the platform we're aiming at – in the case of the Raspberry Pi keyboard is best so we're going to track the left and right arrow keys, along with the space bar for firing laser bolts. Why space? Because it's the convention. How do you know? By playing games. If you ever needed an excuse for trying out as many games as possible you can now do it in the name of research!

Other inputs during the game will include buttons for starting, choosing levels, exiting and help.

Output

Think about how the user will experience the game. First and foremost, they'll see the fruit, laser and bullets appear on-screen and then move. So we'll need to write code for both displaying these graphical elements and animating them. The player also needs to see a score and any other status information we plan to build in – perhaps a time limit and basic instructions – so we'll need to find a way to display information in text format. And then we'll need to write code to play the obligatory bleeps of the classic arcade game.

But output isn't just what the player sees or hears. If we want to store the player's high scores we need to save the data somewhere – this is also output even though it's not visible to the user.

Logic

Whilst the player might notice the quality of graphics and animations or how well the laser gun responds to their keyboard presses, far more effort will go into the behind-the-scenes tasks our program must carry out to make sure the game works as intended. Logic is the glue that links Input to Output, without it you might have falling fruit and rising bullets but no way of connecting the two which is, after all, the point of a game.

In most cases, you'll find yourself spending the majority of your time writing logic code. For example we must constantly send new co-ordinates for all the objects on the screen to the output code so that it can accurately reflect their positions. We must check for collisions and, when they happen, react accordingly by updating the output and scores as well as checking whether the game has finished. By breaking these down into smaller and smaller steps, you eventually end up at the level of the single programming task.

Mirror Mirror

Most programs interact with a user in some way. With a game, it's the user that's providing the input in the first place. In fact, the player and the program become part of a cycle – the user sees the fruit descending (input), decides where to move the laser gun (logic) and presses the keys accordingly (output). Put another way, the output of your computer program becomes the player's input, and vice versa.

If you're designing a program that interacts with a user in this way, you must take account of the whole system – it's not enough to think about the best way for the code to accept input, you must also consider how the player can best provide it. For example, when choosing the best keys for moving the gun left and right, it may be more convenient from a programming point of view to choose A and B but it makes much more sense for the user to use the left and right arrow keys. We've all used apps that have clearly been designed for the convenience of the programmer – just remember that frustration when you come to create your own.

Modularise

So you've split the tasks your program needs to perform into input, logic and output – but how does this translate into the real world of creating your game? It does this by helping you to work out how to organise your code. Imagine slicing a pie into equal parts – you could begin by cutting it into thirds, and then continuing to halve until you reach the optimum size. Input, logic and output are these thirds which you then divide up into smaller units of programming.

In Python these units are called **Modules**, **Functions** and **Objects**.

Modules

To create a Python program, you type code into an editor and save it. The saved file is a module so, in a way, every Python program could be called a module, even our tiny clock. However, typing all your code into a single file is rarely a good idea unless the app is very simple. More typically, you create a main script file and then split the rest of the code into separate files – each of which is a module. For example, you might create a module for handling the display, one for saving the score and reading it back and another to listen for the user's key presses. You would then make the code in those modules available to the main script by "importing" them.

Take a look again at the first line of the clock code:

```
import time, pygame
```

As you've probably guessed, *time* and *pygame* are modules. *time* is built into all Python installations and is, in effect, part of the standard language whereas *pygame* is a specialised module that helps in the development of games. Importing your own modules is done in exactly the same way.

Functions

Modules are broken down into Functions – blocks of code that perform a specific task and have their own unique name. For example, in the "display" module for our game, we might have a function for drawing the bullet onto the screen, another for painting the animated background and a third for exploding the fruit. It's within these functions that you'll find the lines of code that make up the program – so functions are the smallest subdivision.

Objects

Python is an *Object Oriented programming language* in contrast to *Procedural* languages such as most variants of BASIC. In a nutshell this means that the code that controls how parts of a program works is contained within those parts rather than in a big central file. A procedural program is like a puppeteer, pulling the strings from outside whereas an object oriented version would put the intelligence inside the puppet so all the puppeteer would do is give it instructions. Why is this better? Firstly because the code for the puppet and puppeteer is separated out so each can be built and maintained independently. Even more usefully, if we want a second puppet we simply copy the first as many times as we like whereas a puppeteer soon runs out of arms!

Think about a game of Space Invaders. The invaders themselves are identical to each other and move left, right and down the screen. The procedural approach would be to draw each invader separately, one at a time and to keep track in memory of which one is where, whether it's been destroyed or has reached the bottom of the screen. The object oriented approach is to write code for one invader (this is called a Class) so that it keeps track of its own position and status, and then to create as many copies (called Instances) of that class as necessary. Once they're up and running, they each run independently. As a rule OOP means less code overall, programming that is much easier to understand when you go back to it (as you know that any code within the Invader class relates to the aliens) and, because of this faster programming, fewer bugs and better performance.

So, a Python program is usually made up of *modules* containing *functions* and *classes* (which also contain functions). Despite their somewhat intimidating names modules, functions and classes are essentially just ways of organising code so they're there to make life easier. With that behind us, it's time to dive into Python.

Part 3

PROGRAMMING IN PYTHON

Programming in Python

It's time to dive into Python itself and learn the basic skills needed to create Python programmes. During this section, you'll find many code samples. These are all short and I strongly recommend that you type them in because this will reinforce your learning and give you practice in using an editor and running programs. You can also download the full code from the book's companion website: www.rpilab.net

Don't worry if you struggle with some of the concepts introduced in this section – I cover a lot of ground very quickly because I want to move onto programming our projects as quickly as possible. Whether you're aware of it or not, if you follow the examples, most of what you need to know will sink in and you'll then have plenty of opportunity to see how the fundamentals of Python work in action as we build the code for the projects in the next parts of the book.

Introducing Python

All programming languages have the same broad purpose – to give a way for humans to control devices powered by a microprocessor. With most languages, code made up of letters, numbers and symbols is typed into an editor line by line before being run by the computer.

Python is a high level language because the code itself is relatively English-like – indeed any competent programmer looking at a well designed Python application would be able to work out what it was trying to achieve, whether or not they'd ever learned the language itself. As you can imagine, this makes Python a good first language and, indeed, an excellent choice for a wide range of purposes.

Human and machine languages have much in common. Perhaps the biggest difference is that whilst you don't have to speak perfect German to make yourself understood to a native, computers are entirely unforgiving. This is because, at their digital hearts, computers understand only two conditions - 1 and 0, right and wrong – so there can be none of the ambiguity or guesswork of human communication. Fortunately, Python is much easier to learn than French, for example, and when you get it wrong, only you and your Raspberry Pi knows. And the Pi won't tell.

The Basics

Python is an interpreted language which means there's a separate Python *Interpreter* that, when you run a program, reads the text files you write and converts them into the low level code that the computer understands. Contrast this with C, on the other hand, which is a compiled language. With C, you develop your code and, as part of that process, it's converted into a machine form that doesn't need an interpreter. All things being equal, compiled code runs more quickly than its interpreted equivalent because it's ready to go when it's loaded, whereas Python needs to load its runtime engine first, read in the text files and then run the program.

If that's the case, why do we have interpreted languages? Firstly because the difference in speed is, for most real world purposes, undetectable on modern hardware (even the Raspberry Pi). Sure, if you wanted to create a 3D engine for a first person video game, you'd write that in C (or C++) rather than Python but most games, and most other programs, run perfectly through a runtime engine.

The main benefit of an interpreted language is that it eliminates a step from the development process. With Python you can write code, save it and can immediately run it to see whether it works. With C, you must write, save and compile before you get results. The more code you write, the longer this takes and the more time you save with Python.

I've covered the organisation of the work a computer program does into Input, Logic and Output. In practice this means that Python programs tend to be made up of several text files which are usually give a .py extension. In most cases there is a central file, usually called main.py, which is the starting point – this is the text file that the interpreter is instructed to run. The other files are linked to main.py using the *import* statement and if you could slow the interpreter down to human reading speed, you'd be able to watch as it jumps in and out of those other files in response to your commands, but always returning back to main.py. Geany makes all this very easy because it has a button on the toolbar for running the project – just make sure you have main.py in the edit window when you click!

The Python Philosophy

Very few programmers stick to a single language and, as you become more experienced you'll notice that each has a "personality" of its own. Quite often, you'll prefer one language over another because its personality appeals to you, so it's good news that Python is easy to like.

As you'd expect from a language that takes its name from a TV comedy series, Python doesn't take itself too seriously. Some languages seem to hoard their secrets and so attract fans who take great pride in overcoming their limitations – the harder it is to get something done, the more they seem to like it. Python takes the opposite approach and so it's built a community of fans eager to help others get into the language.

The Zen of Python

1: There is one right way to do it

Some languages encourage you to find your own way of achieving something, providing many different methods. Whilst Python has plenty of flexibility when it comes to organising your code (which is your business), when it comes to writing individual lines of code to carry out a task, there's usually a single best way to go about it. If it feels as though you're going around the houses to get something done, there's almost certainly a better way.

2: Always choose simple over complex and complex over complicated

Python is built to make it easy for you to write simple code. This is good because it reduces bugs and makes it simpler to maintain your program whether you're doing it or someone else. If you can't make it simple then make it complex but clear rather than complicated.

3: Get it done

Python is an incredibly productive language. It takes a remarkably small amount of code to achieve useful results. Whereas programmers using other languages boast about how many lines of code their application contains, Python programmers brag about how few lines it took

4: Organise for readability

As you'll see in the next chapters, Python includes many ways of putting code into blocks to get things done. You can also put blocks within blocks (within blocks) but this leads to dense, difficult to understand code. If this happens when writing Python code, you need to think about how you can put the sub-blocks elsewhere (for example into modules, functions or objects) so that the main code remains simple to read and understand.

5: Have fun

Whereas coding in some languages can feel as though you're wading through treacle to do the simplest things -Objective-c and Java, I'm looking at you- using Python is a joy. If you don't have fun writing programs using Python then you might want to reconsider being a programmer. As with any new skill, learning to program is a challenge but Python makes it as simple as possible whilst doing its best to demand little and deliver plenty.

No Curly Braces

If you've seen programming code at any point, you've probably seen curly braces used to divide code into blocks. When the interpreter reaches an opening curly brace { it knows that everything that follows belongs together, until it gets to a closing brace }. The problem with this approach is that you end up with a lot of curly braces! Traditionally, programmers have used tab indenting to make a visual link – in other words all the code that's indented by the same number of tab stops belongs together. However, most languages use the braces to group code so using tab stops is purely optional and anything that's optional tends to get forgotten by busy programmers. The end result is a mess of braces that can be very difficult to understand.

Python solves this problem by not using curly braces at all but relying entirely on indentation. In other words, if you don't organise your code to be easy to read, it won't work at all but code that does work is, by definition, readable. Remember, then, that you must take care with indenting. It becomes natural very quickly but it's also the biggest single source of errors by new coders, especially those transferring across from another language.

Python Basics: Statements and Expressions

We've looked at how programs are split, like a book, into smaller and smaller subdivisions. When you're planning a novel, you need to think about the overall plot, character and setting but actually writing the book is done one word at a time, building up into sentences, paragraphs, pages and chapters. Planning a program involves thinking about what you want to achieve through Input-Logic-Output and how that's reflected in its modules, objects and functions but it boils down to typing code letter by letter into an editor.

The programming equivalent of the sentence is called a *statement* – it's the smallest chunk of code that makes sense on its own. Statements are usually made up of several expressions which you can think of as similar to verbs in that they get things done. They achieve this by creating and using objects, whether these are built-into Python or created separately (perhaps by you). One of the main advantages of Python over other, lower level, languages is the sheer range of pre-existing objects each with its own purpose. If you were a C programmer you'd spend much of your time manually setting up the objects used in your application, using Python allows you to bypass much of this and get on with making something useful quickly.

Start up Geany

We're going to look at some simple code and the best possible way for you to learn is to follow along. To do this, start up Geany and click the *Terminal* tab in the *Message* window at the bottom. If you don't see the Message window at all, click the *View* menu, and select the *Show Message Window* option. If *Terminal* is not amongst the tabs and you're using Linux then open up a Terminal window and type the following line to install it.

```
sudo apt-get install libvte9
```

Now, restart Geany and the tab should appear. If it doesn't then use LXTerminal (on the Raspberry Pi) or the Terminal app in other forms of Linux. If you're using Windows, you'll need to run the command prompt.

In all cases, now type "python" into the Terminal tab (or window) to start the Python interpreter. You should get a message reporting which version of Python is running, followed by the prompt >>> which indicates that it's waiting for input. What's happening here is that you are talking directly to the interpreter rather than loading a text file into it. This means you can try things out instantly, which is what we're going to do now.

Note: in the code snippets that follow, if I want you to type code into the interpreter via the Terminal/Command Prompt, I'll start the line with >>>. Lines that don't begin with the chevrons represent text the interpreter is "printing" out and should not be typed.

Variables

In basic algebra, you swap numbers for letters to help solve problems. For example:

a x 3 = 6

where, in this case, *a* is equal to 2. Variables work in a similar way – they act as containers for values. These values can be numbers, letters or even objects – the variable works as a convenient way of working on a value and passing it from place to place.

Let's look at this by re-writing the above code as it might appear in a real program. Go to the Terminal tab in Geany (or a running Terminal or Command Prompt) and type the following lines, pressing Enter after each (don't type the chevrons!):

```
>>> a=2

>>> print(a * 3)

6
```

The first line creates a variable called *a* and gives it a value of 2. The second line is a statement that contains an object (*print*) and an expression (*a * 3*).

What makes the last part an *expression* is that it returns a value that it has calculated. In this case, Python multiplies the variable *a* (which contains a value of 2 as set in the previous line) by 3 giving a result of 6. Note that in programming, we use the asterisk to indicate multiplication.

The result is sent to the print object which, as you'll have guessed already, simply writes the value to the message window. You should see the number appear on the next line.

Here's a variation:

```
>>> a = 2
>>> b = 3
>>> print(a * b)

6
```

You'll see the number 6 appear again, just as before. This time two variables were multiplied together.

Let's try a simple VAT calculator. Type the following and press enter:

```
>>>beforeVAT=raw_input("Add VAT to this: ")
```

raw_input is a Python function that asks the user to type something in. In this case we add a message asking them to tell us what figure they want us to add VAT to. This figure is then assigned to the variable *beforeVAT*.

When you see the prompt, type a number (for example 100) and press enter. Then type the following, pressing enter after each line:

```
>>>afterVAT=float(beforeVAT)*1.2
>>>print(afterVAT)
```

The second line creates a new variable, *afterVAT* which is the result of *beforeVAT* (the number you typed in) multiplied by 1.2 (which has the effect of adding 20%) and, finally, we print this new value out on the next line.

Now, that's all very well but what if we wanted to use this program again? Commands typed into the interpreter will be erased from memory when you shut down your computer or Geany so we're going to start creating files for our programs so we can keep and reuse them.

In Geany, select *File/New* (don't select a template) and type the following line (including the # symbol)

```
#my first program
```

Now Save the file to a location of your choice, making sure you add the extension .py to the end of the file name. You should notice that your single line has turned red. This is because any line that begins with the # symbol is ignored by Python - it's used to make comments in your code so that when you come back to it you can understand what you were doing. Geany knows you're writing Python code because you added .py to the file name, so it's turned the line red to indicate a comment.

Retype all the lines of the VAT calculator into Geany. Notice that, as you type the first few characters of *raw_input*, Geany offers an autocomplete – press Enter to accept. It also shows you what information *raw_input* expects you to type in – this can be very useful to help you learn the specific commands and also reduces bugs.

Once you've typed each line, save the file and then click the *Execute* button on the Geany toolbar (the cogs). After a short delay, LXTerminal will pop up and your prompt will appear. Type a number and Python will tell you what the total including VAT would be.

Now that the program has been saved, you can run it as many times as you like by loading it into Geany and clicking *Execute*

Variable Names

You have plenty of flexibility about what you call your variables. You can use any letter and number (although the first character of a variable cannot be a number – 1ucy for example) and also the underscore character. There are a few words that Python uses itself ("else" for example) which you can't use but don't worry too much, it'll soon tell you!

The Python community uses some conventions which, in the main, I'll follow in this book but, in the end, whatever system you use needs to make sense to you. You can't use spaces in variable names as they must all be one word. One way to get around this is to use the underscore character, another is to capitalise the first letter of words after the first – this is called camelCase. It's up to you whether you believe that my_variable is a better name than myVariable, Python doesn't mind – both are more readable than myvariable though. For now, don't sweat it – just try to be consistent.

Data

We've seen that we can use variables as containers and then do things with them. In the example so far, we've used numbers but Python provides several types that you'll be using a lot. Here are the most important:

Numbers

Which of the following are numbers?

```
3290, 3290.123, 3290e3, "3290"
```

We can find out by making use of the fact that Python is a strongly typed language. This means that if you try to, for example, multiply two variables that are not both numbers, it will throw an error. PHP, which is another popular programming language (and one I like very much), on the other hand, would do its best to work out what you meant but this can often result in bugs.

Go back to the Geany Terminal tab and type:

```
>>> a=3290; print(a*5)
```

```
16450
```

Python prints the answer we'd expect. Notice that semi-colon? It's there to allow us to put two statements on one line. Other languages use the semi-colon at the end of every line, in Python we only use it when we want to use multiple statements on a single line.

Now let's try the next one:

```
>>> a=3290.123; print(a*5)
```

```
16450.615
```

This time, the number has a decimal point – in Python numbers formatted like this are called *floats* because they have a floating point. Numbers (such as in the first example) without points are called *integers*. Floats take up a little more memory than integers so only use them if you need the extra precision. Note that when two number types are multiplied (the floating point 3290.123 and the integer 5), Python shows the answer in the most precise form – in this case as a float.

Back to the terminal:

```
>>>a=3290e3; print(a*5)
```

```
16450000.0
```

This is another type of floating point number, except that this time we used e3 at the end to create the equivalent of 3290 x 1000 or, put another way 3290000.0.

Now try:

```
>>>a="3290"; print(a*5)
```

```
32903290329032903290
```

That was unexpected! But completely logical - to Python. By putting quotes around the number, you told Python that the characters 3290 were intended to be treated as a string rather than a number. A string is a sequence of letters, numbers and symbols intended to be treated as text. When you multiply a string, as we did here, Python thinks you want multiple copies so it just repeats them.

To see Python throw a real wobbler, try this slightly different version (with a plus rather than a multiplication symbol):

```
>>>a="3290"; print(a+5)
```

What happens? Give it a try. Python shows an error message because the + symbol means different things depending on whether it's dealing with numbers, where it means to add the numbers together arithmetically, and strings, where it means glue the second onto the end of the first. So, "raspberry " + "pi" becomes "raspberry pi" whereas "raspberry " + 3.141592 (the number pi) would cause an error.

Although Python has several other number types, most of the time you'll stick to integers and floats. As you've seen, to perform arithmetic on numbers, we use the * operator to represent "multiplied by" and + to indicate addition. We can also process numbers in different ways using built in functions and modules – the most useful being the *math* module. Yes, I know, it should be *maths* - that's how Monty Python would spell it!

Of the operators, *modulus* is probably the only one that's not immediately obvious. It's simply the remainder left after long division. So, 11%2 gives a result of 1 because 2 goes into 11 five times with 1 left over, this is the modulus. You'd be surprised at how often this is used in programming – it's excellent for finding out if a number is odd or even because any even number divided by 2 will have a modulus of 0, whereas any odd number divided by 2 always results in a modulus of 1. You might use this, for example, when shading the rows of a table alternately. It's also often used in error checking - the last digit of a book's ISBN is a check digit which is the remainder (or modulus) of division operations on the other digits.

Now for a few of the more useful and interesting functions of the *math* module. Python has two types of built in function, those such as *round* that can be used as if they were part of the language and those, like *math.floor* that can only be used if the appropriate module is imported first. Don't worry, it's very simple – take a look at these. Remember, they're still all one line:

math.floor

Always rounds down to the nearest integer

```
>>>import math; a=9.0; b=a/5; print math.floor(b)

1.0
```

math.ceil

Always rounds up to the nearest integer

```
>>>import math; a=9.0; b=a/5; print math.ceil(b)

2.0
```

math.pi

Stores the value of pi

```
>>>import math; print math.pi

3.14159265359
```

It's Maths – but don't panic!!

If the idea of having to deal with maths brings you out in a cold sweat, there's good news. Far from being the difficult to grasp subject you might have found it at school, maths is at the heart of all computer programming so you'll get to see its practical use. And the good news is that the vast majority of all the maths-related programming you'll ever do is based on simple arithmetic.

Strings

For the most part, strings in programming are plain English words. Strings are used to store usernames, text we're going to display onscreen (for example the prompt we used earlier with *raw_input*) and text we want to work with – database fields for example.

To tell Python you want a variable to be a string, you simply enclose the text in double or single quotes. It really makes no difference which you choose, as long as you only select one or the other for any particular string.

These are equally valid:

```
>>>myName="Terry"
```

```
>>>myName='Terry'
```

...but this will throw an error because single quotes are used at the start and double at the end:

```
>>>myName='Terry"
```

What if the string has speech marks or apostrophes? Here's what you do:

```
>>>myName="Terry's Teriffics"
```

or

```
>>>myName='Terry "Terrific" Travis"
```

In other words, if the string contains apostrophes, surround it with double quotes and vice versa. Given that apostrophes and single quotes turn up in text more often than speech marks, it makes sense to use double quotes by default.

Hold on, what if a piece of text contains both? In that case, add a backslash in front of the character you've used to enclose the string where it appears within the text. So, in this case we want Python to jump over the apostrophe and carry on to the single quote at the end.

```
>>>myName='Terry\'s the "Terrific" Travis'
```

Things to do with Strings

Once you've loaded some text into your variable to create a string, Python allows you to process it in all sorts of weird and wonderful ways. Python thinks of strings as being similar to Scrabble tiles – each character on its own tile – which makes it really easy to get at any letter or number, as well as dead simple to split the string into bits.

len

Tells us how long a string is (including spaces)

```
>>>print len("Terry Travis")

12
```

+

Add (concatenate) two strings together

```
>>>print "Terry " + "Travis"

Terry Travis
```

String[position]

Return the character at that position in the string (the first position is zero)

```
>>>a="Terry Travis"; print a[0]

T
```

String[p1:p2]

Return all the characters between two positions

```
>>>a="Terry Travis"; print a[5:12]

Travis
```

replace(old,new)

Replaces an existing set of characters with another

```
>>>a="Terry Travis"; print a.replace("rav","ard")

Terry Tardis
```

split

Splits a string into parts

```
>>>a="Terry Travis"; print a.split()

['Terry', 'Travis']
```

Lists

Strings and numbers contain single values – Python's list object allows you to store multiple values in one variable. Imagine, for example, you had a database of names like "Terry Travis" and you wanted to write letters to everyone using their first name only. The names could be stored in a list object then pulled out one at a time so that the split() function could be used to fetch the first name from each.

Here's how that list of names might look:

```
>>>list_of_names=['Andrew Ant','Charlie Childs','Martina
Mongoose','Peter Purbrook','Terry Travis','Vera Verity']
```

To pull out Terry we could do this:

```
>>>this_name=list_of_names[4]
```

```
>>>print "Full name="+this_name
```

```
Full name=Terry Travis
```

To isolate just his first name:

```
>>>first_name=this_name.split()[0]
```

```
>>>print "First name="+first_name
```

```
First name=Terry
```

Bear in mind that in Python, and most other computer languages, when you're selecting elements from inside a variable, the numbering starts with 0 not 1 as you might expect. This number is called an *index* and the item it fetches is called an *element*. In the case of a string, specifying a single index gives you one character from the string as its element whereas with a list, you get the whole element. So, *"Terry Travis"[0]* would return "T" (the first character), whereas *list_of_names[0]* would give you "Andrew Ant".

A list can contain a mix of variables, including other lists. For example, imagine a calendar divided into the weeks of the year- each of these weeks would be a list containing the dates. For example, this is how it would look for the beginning of 2016:

```
>>>year_2016=[[31,1,2,3,4,5,6],[7,8,9,10,11,12,13],[14,1
5,16,17,18,19,20],[21,22,23,24,25,26,27],[28,29,30,31,
1,2,3]]
```

```
>>>week=year_2016[1]
```

```
>>>print week
```

```
[7, 8, 9, 10, 11, 12, 13]
```

Note how each of the nested lists is contained within square brackets. The second line fetches the dates for the second week in January (remember, list indexes start with 0] – a list within a list. You could extract the date for Wednesday of that week with week[2].

As you can see, lists allow you to pack a lot of data into a single variable. Don't worry if they seem a little complex, at the moment, we'll be using lists a lot and you'll soon get to grips with them.

Dictionaries

You can think of dictionaries as super-lists. Like lists, they're collections of other objects but unlike lists each element is given its own name so you can access the variable directly. Try this:

```
>>>      family={'father':'Terry',      'mother':'Vera',
'daughter':'Jane', 'son':'Jack'}

>>> print family['father']

Terry
```

As you can see, each pair is given a name and a value – we can then pull out any dictionary element by using that name. As you'd expect, this means that each name must be used only once per dictionary. You'll also notice that dictionaries use curly braces to indicate when they start and end whereas lists use square brackets – this is how Python knows which of the two you mean to create.

You can change the contents of both lists and dictionaries during a program. If you typed in the family example above, you could change it like this:

```
>>>family['son']='Jak'

>>>print family['son']

Jak
```

You don't have to use literal values when you create a dictionary or list – you can use a variable instead.

```
>>>son="Jake"

>>>family['son']=son

>>>print family['son']

Jake
```

This time, we created a new variable called son and assigned it a string value "Jake". We can then use the variable to feed into the family dictionary. Not particularly useful as it stands, but imagine if we were reading a database of families – we'd then be able to change the son variable to the name of each son without having to type them manually.

Finally, you can add a new entry to a dictionary after it's been created – in this case let's add grandparents:

```
>>>family['grandad']='Cyril'

>>>family['granny']='Edith'

>>>print family

{'daughter': 'Jane', 'grandad': 'Cyril', 'mother':
'Vera', 'father': 'Terry', 'son': 'Jake', 'granny':
'Edith'}
```

If you've ever used another programming language, you'll probably have come across arrays. In that case, you've probably already worked out that lists and dictionaries are the equivalent Python structures. Where you might have used a standard array sorted by index in PHP, for example, you use the list in Python. Dictionaries are the equivalent of associative arrays in other languages. If you've never programmed before, just bear this in mind when you look at the documentation for other languages – this is one aspect in which Python is quite unusual.

Fortune Teller

http://scrib.me/fteller

```
1  import random
2  fortunes=['Yes','Probably','Certainly','Outlook promising','Not sure',
   'Ask again','Doubtful','No']
3  how_many_fortunes=len(fortunes)
4  raw_input('Think of a question, press Enter for the answer')
5  which_fortune=random.randint(0,how_many_fortunes-1)
6  print fortunes[which_fortune]
```

Remember those little plastic balls that presented a random answer to your questions when you shook them? Let's create our own Fortune Teller in Python – in just a few lines of code. We're going to want to run this more than once so fire up Geany and type in the listing you'll find at the above URL (as with all other code samples, if you're using an ereader such as a Kindle, I recommend scanning the QR Code above and viewing the code on a tablet or large-screen smartphone or using the shortcode in your browser).

The code begins by importing the *random* module which will allow us to pick one of the answers randomly each time the program is run. On line 2 we create a list containing all 8 of the possible answers (feel free to change them as you wish).

On line 3 we use the *len* function to find out how many answers there are. This might seem unnecessary because we could simply count them (*how_many_fortunes*=8), but by doing it this way we can add and remove answers at any point without affecting the rest of the code.

Line 4 pauses the program, displays the prompt and waits for the user to press the enter key.

In line 5 we use the *randint* function to generate a number. Notice the brackets after *randint*? Those are there to pass parameters to *randint*. Parameters are the bits of information the function needs to work. In this case, we're telling *randint* to generate a number between 0 and *how_many_fortunes-1*. Given that there are 8 fortunes in our example, this means *randint* will give us a number between 0 and 7. We need this because, in case you've forgotten, the first item in a list has an index of 0, not 1 as you might expect. Therefore, the last one has an index of 7, not 8. Don't worry if you find this a little frustrating, the zero-based indexing of lists and other similar objects catches out the most experienced programmers from time to time.

Finally, on line 6 we print the element from *fortune* that has the index generated by *randint*.

Run the program a couple of times by clicking the cogs to make sure the randomness is working – you should get a different answer pretty much every time. Also have a go at changing the text in the answers and adding or removing some.

Congratulations – you have just written your first fully functional computer programme – a fortune ball in 6 lines!

Making Decisions and getting things done

Over 200 years ago Joseph Jacquard demonstrated a new mechanical loom with a unique feature – it used punched cards to control the pattern of the textile the loom was creating. Each card contained several rows of holes in specific locations. As the card is fed through row by row, small rods detect whether there is a hole – if there is, that particular thread will be used, if not it won't. Since each row has 25-30 positions for holes, very complex patterns can be created with minimal human involvement. Load up another set of cards, and you get a completely different pattern.

Jacquard's invention (building on earlier work by others) was such an efficient way to create textiles that it's still in wide use today. It also gave rise to two important concepts that formed the foundation of computing - the idea that you can program a series of operations in advance and, secondly, that a machine can be given more than one purpose by simply changing its "software" (or "paperware" in this case).

If you were to take one row of holes from a set of Jacquard cards, and represented holes with a 1 and the absence of a hole with 0, you might get a sequence like this:

111110011000001100111001111111111

In other words, they used the nineteenth century equivalent of binary notation – the "language" at the heart of all digital computers. The looms used mechanics in place of programming languages but, essentially they worked in a similar way – if a 1 was encountered in any particular position, a certain action was taken, if it wasn't then either a different action was taken or nothing happened.

Jacquard's system had only one variable type (a binary number) whereas Python has many (including its equivalent of the binary type – the Boolean). We've covered the most important of these –

numbers, strings, lists and dictionaries – now it's time to move onto the coding equivalent of the mechanics that decide what to do with those variables.

If-Then?

The ability to make decisions based on the contents of variables and then take actions depending on the results is what separates computers from calculators and *if-then-else* is the most important decision-making structure. In the case of the Jacquard loom, each position on the card where there might be a hole is a simple if-statement. In English this could be written as:

If there's a hole here then use the blue thread otherwise use the yellow thread.

In Python, that statement might be represented as:

```
if hole==1:

    thread=blue

else:

    thread=yellow
```

The first thing you'll notice is how clear it is – you could work out that it intended without any knowledge of Python. Indeed, this sort of easy readability is one of the main aims of the language. We begin with the *if* keyword, and we follow this with the condition that is being tested. In this case, if the hole variable (a number) is equal to 1 then the program moves immediately to the next line. You'll notice that this line is indented and Python will now carry out all lines at that indentation (in this case there is only one). If the hole variable is not 1 then the interpreter skips down to the line containing *else* and executes the code beneath it.

Python uses a colon to indicate the start of a block of code and then continues until the indentation changes. In practice what this means is that you add the colon, then hit the return key to start a new line. You then tab once (Geany does this automatically after a colon) and type your first line – every other line that's also tabbed once will be executed one after another. The interpreter will stop when it spots a different indentation.

This is really important – *Python is the only mainstream language that relies entirely on indentation to mark blocks of code.* The benefit of this is that your code is much clearer as I explained earlier but it takes a little getting used to. Let's look at a slightly more involved chunk of code to make sure you understand.

names.py

```
1    input_name=raw_input("What is your name? ")
2    name_length=len(input_name)
3    average_name_length=5
4
5    if name_length>average_name_length:
6        result="longer"
7        conjunction="than"
8    elif name_length<average_name_length:
9        result="shorter"
10       conjunction="than"
11   else:
12       result="the same"
13       conjunction="length as"
14
15   response=input_name+", your name is "+result+" "+conjunction+" "+
     "average"
16   print response
```

http://scrib.me/namespy

This little program asks the user to type in their name, it then works out how many characters their name contains. The *if* block compares this with the average length of a first name (the *average_name_length* variable) and puts together a response depending on the result.

On line 5, the length of the user's name is compared to the average. If their name length is greater than the average (we use the > symbol from maths), then the code on lines 6 and 7 is carried out. Once Python reaches the end of the red text, it jumps out of the *if* statement and straight down to line 15.

If their name length is not greater than average, the interpreter skips to line 8. *elif* is short for "else if" – in other words "now check whether this is true". This time, we ask whether their name length is less than (<) the average – if it is, the code on lines 9 and 10 is carried out and Python then jumps down to line 15.

If the user's name is neither larger nor smaller than the average, it must be the same length. So, we use *else* as a catch-all – it means "if none of the others is true, then do this". Bear in mind that Python will only arrive at this line if it hasn't already been diverted by one of the other if statements – this time it will carry out the instructions on lines 12 and 13 before jumping to line 15.

Give it a try – with names of different lengths to make sure it works.

We've now met three different ways to compare two variables: equals (==), less than (<) and greater than (>). The complete list of commonly used comparison operators is shown here:

```
==
```

Are the two values the same?

```
if a==b:
```

```
<
```

Is the first value less than the second?

```
if a<b:
```

```
>
```

Is the first value more than the second?

```
if a>b:
```

```
>=
```

Is the first value greater than or equal to the second?

```
if a>=b:
```

`<=`

Is the first value less than or equal to the second?

```
if a<=b:
```

`!=`

or

`<>`

Is the first value not equal to the second?

```
if a!=b:
```

Finally, in case you were wondering, we use == rather than = for "equals" in conditional statements because Python assigns values to variables using =. Watch out for this – it'll trip you up sooner or later!

Repeating yourself

You could think of *if-then-else* as the brains of the outfit – in which case the two main looping structures in Python (*while* and *for*) are its muscles and heart. After all, making a decision on its own would lead to very short programs. The Jacquard Loom only worked because the cards were constantly fed into the machine via a loop mechanism, otherwise it would only have created one line of thread.

Remember our fortune teller app? Every time you wanted to ask a new question, you were forced to run the program again. Loops avoid this by allowing you to run code multiple times and almost every useful Python program will include them.

for..in

If you want to do something a specific number of times, the *for* loop is the tool to pick. Let's take a look at a very simple for loop in action

```
input_name=raw_input("What is your name?")

for c in input_name:
    print c
```

Give it a go – create a Python file in Geany, type in these three lines and run it. When prompted, enter your name. You'll find that Python then prints each character of your name one at a time, each on a separate line.

The structure of a **for** loop is this:

```
for [iterator] in [collection]:
```

collection means any variable that can be split into parts – lists and dictionaries are often used but in this example, it's a string. *iterator* is just the name we give to each bit as it's pulled out. Put into English, our example would be "for each letter in input_name" and it means that the next line will be repeated until it gets to the end of the collection (the name you typed in, in this example)

So, let's say you typed "Jo Bloggs" at the prompt. *Collection* is therefore *"Jo Bloggs"* and the loop will start. The value of *iterator* will be *"J"* to start with and so the print line will output that letter. Python now checks to see if we've reached the end of the collection and, since we haven't, moves to the next letter and prints *"o"*.

Bear in mind that if there were several lines after the *for* statement, Python would execute them all as part of the loop – until it got to a line that wasn't in the same tab position, at which point it would go back to the for and start again.

What do you think would happen if you replaced the first line with this? Give it a try.

```
input_name=("Jo", "Bloggs")
```

You should find that, this time, Python prints "Jo" on one line and "Bloggs" on the next rather than each word on its own line. Why? Because *input_name* is now a list, not a string, so the iterator is now each element in the list, not the individual characters in the string. In fact, it's much more common to iterate over a list than a string – largely because lists are so useful.

If you've studied any other programming language, you've probably come across a *for* structure that iterates a fixed number of times – in BASIC this would be written as for n=1 to 10 – this would create a loop that ran 10 times. Whilst this might seem simpler, in practice you will find that you nearly always iterate through a collection so the Python approach is much more efficient. However, sometimes you do need to loop a fixed number of times – for example if you wanted to create a specific number of objects – so this is the equivalent of that BASIC statement:

```
for n in range(10):
```

Again, simply indent the code you want to be run ten times (in this case) by one tab stop.

while

Most Python programs , especially games, include the *while* loop. In English, this loop means "while a particular condition is satisfied, keep looping". For example, in a game, you will usually have a main loop that keeps repeating until the escape key is pressed.

View the code

```
 1  import random
 2  user_roll=raw_input("What number did you roll?")
 3  my_roll=0
 4  how_many_rolls=0
 5
 6  while my_roll != int(user_roll):
 7      my_roll=random.randint(1,6)
 8      how_many_rolls+=1
 9      print my_roll
10
11  print "it took "+str(how_many_rolls)+" rolls"
```

http://scrib.me/randomdice

This little program asks you to roll a dice and input the number, it then works out how many rolls it took to get the same number (on average it should be around 6). As you can see, we need to begin by importing the *random* module. We also create two number variables and set them to zero.

When Python gets to the *while* loop, it checks its value for *my_roll* (remember, we set it to zero when we created it) and compares that to the number you entered. The *!=* comparison means "does not equal" so, if the *my_roll* does not equal the user's number Python will move into the block. Since you will have typed a number from 1-6, *my_roll* will not *equal user_roll* the first time, so Python will always run the loop at least once.

We then set *my_roll* to a randomly generated number between 1 and 6 to simulate our dice roll. On the next line we increase the *how_many_rolls* variable by 1 to keep track of the number of rolls it took to get the same number the user rolled. The += characters are used as a shorthand to increase (increment) that value by 1.

We then print the randomly generated die roll. Python now jumps back to the *while* line – this time *my_roll* will *not* be zero, it will be a number from 1 to 6. Python checks whether this randomly generated number matches whatever the user typed in earlier. If it doesn't, it moves into the loop again – this continues until they do match, each time generating and printing out a new random number. When it does match, Python jumps to the final line and prints out the number of attempts it took.

You'll notice that the *while* statement includes the *int* function. This is because, when we use *raw_input*, the user's input is treated as a string, even if they've typed in numbers. Python cannot compare a number with a string (even if that string looks like a number) so we use the *int* function to convert the string into an integer (a number without a decimal point) that the while statement can use to compare.

Similarly, on the final line, we use the *str* function to turn the *how_many_rolls* number variable into a string so it can be incorporated into the print statement.

Decisions, Loops, nesting and breaks

Loops and if-then-else structures are at their most powerful when they work together. You can also create loops within loops (this is called nesting) and ifs within ifs – and any combination of both. Indeed a program of any complexity at all will involve these sorts of combinations and it can be tricky to work out where you are at any one time. But this is where Python's clear structure pays off – you know that all lines at the same tab stop are at the same level. This is much easier than the approach other languages use of employing curly braces – in that case, unless you've been hyper-careful making sure your tabs line up, you'll end up counting braces to see where you are. In Python, if you don't line your tabs up, the program won't work so you're forced to get it right – this is a good thing!

Occasionally, you will want to break out of a loop before it has completed. If you'd created a space invaders game, for example, and were using a *while* loop to update the position of the invaders several times a second, you might want to exit to another part of the program if the user pressed F1 for help. In that case, you use the *break* statement – this exits the loop immediately and proceeds as if it had completed.

The *continue* statement, on the other hand, skips straight back to the start of the loop, preventing Python from executing the remaining lines in that cycle.

Organising your code – functions, objects and modules

We've covered Python's most important nuts and bolts - variables, decisions and loops – enough to create simple programs. However, to create a useful application, you need a way to organise your code, otherwise it would end up as one long, indecipherable, block of Python.

To use a book analogy, functions are the equivalent of paragraphs – a chunk of lines with a specific purpose. Functions can exist on their own or within objects or modules, they're the smallest unit in the Python universe.

Functions

A function, then, is a block of code with a particular purpose. By organising your code this way, it can be used as many times as you like from within your program. For example, you might have a function that reads the system clock every second to update the elapsed time in a game. Rather than having several lines of code to do this within the main program it can be isolated into a function to be called as often as you like. This has the added benefit of making our main code much simpler and easier to understand because it isn't so cluttered. Each function can be named which, again, makes the program as a whole much easier to understand.

Let's get straight into a practical example. Type the following listing into Geany and run it

```
1    import pygame,random
2    pygame.init()
3    clock = pygame.time.Clock() # Clock to limit speed
4    WIDTH=600; HEIGHT=600; BLACK=(0,0,0)
5    screen = pygame.display.set_mode([WIDTH, HEIGHT])
6    screen.fill(BLACK)
7
8    def draw_circle(colour):
9        x=random.randint(1,WIDTH)
10       y=random.randint(1,HEIGHT)
11       size=random.randint(1,5)
12       pygame.draw.circle(screen,colour,(x,y),size)
13
14   def random_colour(minimum, maximum):
15       red=random.randint(minimum,maximum)
16       green=random.randint(minimum,maximum)
17       blue=random.randint(minimum,maximum)
18       colour=[red,green,blue]
19       return colour
20
21   for n in range(100):
22       clock.tick(25)
23       colour=random_colour(100,255)
24       draw_circle(colour)
25       pygame.display.update()
26
27   raw_input("Press a key")
```

http://scrib.me/1yg2In7

This simple program fills a black window with randomly generated circles. You'll remember that when we created *if-then-else*, *while* and *for..in* blocks, we started the block with a colon and then indented the code that is to be run. Functions work in exactly the same way.

We use the *def* keyword to define a function. You can see that, in this code, we have two functions which we've called *draw_circle* and *random_colour* – we can use any name that makes sense to us and follows the rules for naming variables.

When the program is run, Python will begin at line 1 and immediately carry out the instructions through to line 6 (note the two variables WIDTH and HEIGHT are in capitals because that is the convention for variables whose values stay the same throughout). When it gets to line 8, it comes across the first function – rather than run the code within the function it's loaded into memory to be used later. The same happens with the second function (*random_color*).

The Python interpreter arrives at line 21 and finds a for..in loop – in this case a loop that will run exactly 100 times since this is how many circles we want to generate. In other words, Python will carry out the code from line 22 to line 25 one hundred times before the loop ends and the interpreter jumps down to line 27 which just waits for a key to be pressed before ending the program.

To run the code in a function we call it – you can see the two ways to do this on lines 23 and 24. The purpose of many functions is to carry out a task and send back the result. Take a wild guess at what line 23 is doing –

```
colour=random_colour(100,255)
```

Yes, we're creating a variable called *colour* and assigning it the value sent back by the function *random_colour*. Note that every single element in this statement was named by me, not Python, so you can choose words that make sense to you so that your code is easy to understand.

But what about the set of brackets at the end? Well, have a look at the function definition on line 14. Immediately after we name the function, we also indicate what information the function needs in order to run – in other words which parameters must be passed to it. In this case, we need a minimum and maximum value for the colour (see *Focus on: Colour* for an explanation of how colour works).

Since our background window is black, we don't want colours that are too strong or too dark. Look back at line 24 and you'll see we're passing 100 to the function as the first parameter (minimum) and 255 as the second parameter (maximum). Each of the first three lines of the function (starting at line 15) generates a random number between minimum and maximum (100 to 255 in this case). The variable names have been chosen to make clear what they represent – however red, green and blue at this point are just number variables and nothing more, their names are to help us remember their purpose. In line 18, we create a new list variable called *colour* containing each of these random values. Again, it's just a list with a convenient name containing three numbers of between 100 and 255 each. Finally, on line 19, the *return* command sends the list back to the line that called it (line 23).

Scope

Hold your horses – why does the variable *colour* appear twice, that can't be right surely? This is because variables, by default, *only exist inside the function that gives birth to them*. So, the variables within the *random_colour* function (*red, green, blue, colour*) can only be accessed by lines of code also inside that function. The colour variable defined at line 23 is not inside *random_colour* so, from its perspective, the one at line 18 doesn't exist – this is why we must return it. Having said that, if a function contains another function, then variables declared in the parent are accessible in the child. This is why *screen*, which is declared in the main code, can be used in *draw_circle*.

On the face of it, you might think it would make more sense to allow every part of a program to see and use variables from every other part but there are two very good reasons why this isn't a good idea. Firstly, each variable takes up memory and, since the variables within a function are there purely to help the function to perform its task, it would be wasteful to keep them "alive" once it has done so – in fact it might cause a program to run out of memory entirely. Secondly, by keeping variables local to their function, we can reuse the variable name in other functions without causing a naming clash. This isn't just a matter of convenience, it also means that we can use reuse functions across lots of programs (including functions written by other people) without worrying about duplicate variable names.

Occasionally, however, you do need to have access to a variable throughout the program and, to achieve this, you simply add the global keyword before the variable is defined:

```
global my_var = 999
```

However, for the reasons given above you should only use global variables when necessary.

So, *random_colour* generates a list with red, green and blue colour values and sends them back to line 23. What happens next? On line

24, we call our other function *draw_circle*. This time the parameter is the colour we just received back from *random_colour*. On lines 9 and 10 we create random numbers between 1 and the width or height of the program window. Most programming languages use a coordinate system with the point at the top left hand corner being 0,0. The x axis is left to right so, on line 9, we generate a horizontal position for our circle. The y axis is top to bottom so line 10 generates a vertical coordinate. Line 11 generates a random number between 1 and 5 which will be the radius of the circle and line 12 uses the *pygame* module to actually draw the circle on the screen. The interpreter reaches the end of line 12, sees that there is no next line on the same tab stop and goes back to line 25 – there is no return statement this time because, well, there's nothing to return!

To make sure you understand, follow the interpreter as it goes once through the loop from line 21:

21,22,23,14,15,16,17,18,19,24,8,9,10,11,12,25

Each of these iterations generates and displays one circle. Python repeats this until 100 have been generated and then drops down to line 27 to finish.

It's quite possible that, at this moment, your brain is smouldering but don't worry, it becomes natural very quickly and this little program contains most of the key concepts you need to understand to become a coder. From here on in, it's question of broadening your knowledge and applying it to more and more sophisticated (and useful) apps.

FOCUS ON: COLOUR

In Python (and most languages) colours are a mix of red, green and blue and the strength of the colour is set by how high a value it is set to. The values range from 0 to 255 – in other words 256 possibilities. This may seem odd – to a human it would make more sense if it were set at 0-100 for example – but it makes complete sense to a computer. Remember that computers, at their heart, use binary notation and 255, in binary, is 11111111, or, put another way, 28 – in other words it's the largest number that can be written in 8 bits or 1 byte of data. So, 0 represents none of that colour and 255 represents 100% of it.

In Python (and most languages) colours are a mix of red, green and blue and the strength of the colour is set by how high a value it is set to. The values range from 0 to 255 – in other words 256 possibilities. This may seem odd – to a human it would make more sense if it were set at 0-100 for example – but it makes complete sense to a computer. Remember that computers, at their heart, use binary notation and 255, in binary, is 11111111, or, put another way, 28 – in other words it's the largest number that can be written in 8 bits or 1 byte of data. So, 0 represents none of that colour and 255 represents 100% of it.

For our Pygame circle, the mixed colour is written as a list of the three channels so pure white would be [0,0,0] – in other words 0% of red, green and blue – and pure black is [255,255,255] with a mid-grey being [128,128,128]. Pure red would be [255,0,0], pure green [0,255,0] and a pure blue would be [0,0,255].

To get other colours, you simply mix the RGB channels. Magenta is [255,0,255] and yellow [255,255,0] whereas [128,64,0] makes a chocolate brown.

Genie has a colour mixer built in which you can use to work out the best values.

Modules

Essentially, modules are simply groups of functions saved in a separate text file and loaded at runtime. In fact all Python files are modules and the usual approach is to have one main module and one or more other modules with specific jobs. So, a word processor might, in addition to its main module, have modules called print.py, save.py and spellcheck.py.

Python comes with a range of standard modules - *random* and *math* are two that we've used already – and there's a huge selection of third party modules (although the quality will, naturally, vary) including *pygame*. You might wonder why Python doesn't simply include maths functions into the main language, as many others do, but it's a matter of efficiency – not all programs will need random or maths functions and so the code is kept as lean as possible by only including the modules necessary to the particular task.

Python's built-in modules are available automatically – you simply use the *import* statement and they become usable. Third party modules (including your own) either have to be specially installed (as with pygame) or saved as .py files where the interpreter can find them – in practice this usually means including them in the same folder as your code.

Let's look at how we might refactor (improve) our colour circle program using modules. http://scrib.me/1xnOs7L

snow.py

```
1   import pygame,display
2   pygame.init()
3   clock = pygame.time.Clock() # Clock to limit speed
4   screen=display.setup()
5
6   for n in range(100):
7       clock.tick(45)
8       colour=display.random_colour(100,255)
9       display.draw_circle(colour,screen)
10      pygame.display.update()
11
12  raw_input("Press a key")
```

display.py

```
1    import pygame, random
2    WIDTH=600; HEIGHT=600; BLACK=(0,0,0)
3
4    def setup():
5        BLACK=(0,0,0)
6        screen = pygame.display.set_mode([WIDTH, HEIGHT])
7        screen.fill(BLACK)
8        return screen
9
10   def draw_circle(colour,screen):
11       x=random.randint(1,WIDTH)
12       y=random.randint(1,HEIGHT)
13       size=random.randint(1,5)
14       pygame.draw.circle(screen,colour,(x,y),size)
15
16   def random_colour(minimum, maximum):
17       red=random.randint(minimum,maximum)
18       green=random.randint(minimum,maximum)
19       blue=random.randint(minimum,maximum)
20       colour=[red,green,blue]
21       return colour
22
```

In a nutshell, we've exported all the functions to do with drawing to the screen to a new module called *display.py*. This was simply a case of creating a new Python file in Geany and pasting the two existing functions into it. We also added the import statements for *pygame* and *random* to the top and moved the *WIDTH* and *HEIGHT* variable assignments to this module since this is where they're used. The only major addition is that we've put all the screen setup code into a function called *setup*.

Back in our original Python file (our main module), having moved the code across to *display.py* we need to make a few other changes. Firstly, we need to import our new module on line 1 (note, we've removed the *random* import because it's not needed for the code in this module). Secondly, we need to call the *setup* function in *display*.

There are a few things to notice here. Firstly, if we want to call a function in another module, we add the name of the module to the beginning so that Python knows where to find it. Secondly, if a function has no parameters, as here, we add empty brackets. Finally, note that the setup function returns a variable called *screen* – this is because this variable is needed by the *draw_circle*. When we created our *setup* function, we put *screen* inside it which means it's no longer accessible by *draw_circle* so we must return it from *setup* to the main program and then, in line 9, we add it as a new parameter to our *draw_circle* code.

Whilst this might seem a bit of a palaver for very little gain, just take a look at snow.py in its new form. Remember this is the main program and, by removing much of the display code to another module, it's now shorter and very clear. After all, we can understand what *draw_circle* and *random_colour* do by their names, we don't need to see the code (unless there's a bug - in which case we know where to look!).

The more sophisticated the program, the more benefit you gain from organising your code into modules – it's a good habit to get into right from the start

A quick class in object-oriented programming

Many introductory books avoid object-oriented development because it's seen as an advanced topic but it's an essential part of modern-day programming and something you'll need to understand if you're to do serious coding, let alone have a career in programming.

Fortunately, it's a pretty simple concept to get your head around and it's very useful, especially for creating games, so I'm going to tackle it head on. I'll leave some of the nitty-gritty to later chapters, for now the point is to understand what we're doing when we use object-oriented programming (OOP) techniques and why.

The Basics

I introduced objects earlier using puppets as a metaphor. A traditional program would write code to control each puppet, an object oriented program would code the puppets themselves.

The code for an object is contained in a *class* – you can think of this as a blueprint. Each time a new object (sometimes called an *instance*) is needed, Python goes to the class and uses it to do so. In other words, if you needed lots of on-screen puppets, you could write just one class and create a for..in loop to create hundreds at once.

One of the main benefits of OOP is *encapsulation*, the concept that everything an object needs to know is contained within its code. You could, in theory at least, take that object and use it in another program without having to change it at all. In this way, objects are similar to modules and, indeed, they're also made up of functions just as modules are (functions are often called methods when they're inside classes). Objects can sit within the main code, within modules, or in a file of their own – the more sophisticated and/or reusable they are, the more likely it is you'll want to store them separately.

Perhaps the most powerful feature of OOP is *inheritance*. Writing a single class for puppets is all very well, but marionettes come in many forms and the code for creating a Pinnochio, for example, would be somewhat different to that used for creating Mr Punch. Inheritance allows you to have a single generic class that contains all the code that is true for most puppets, and child classes based on that generic code that define only what is additional or different.

So, let's say the generic class includes code for drawing a head, arms and legs so, when we come to create the Pinnochio child class, we don't have to write any of that – we simply write new code for his extending nose for example. The same is true of Mr Punch, except that he doesn't have standard puppet legs – in this case, he can override the draw_legs function of the generic class with his own draw_legs function whilst keeping all the rest of the code intact.

One advantage of this is that you, as a coder, only have to write the minimum code. Another is that it becomes very easy to create new child classes since most of the work is already done. Finally, each change you make to the generic class is immediately inherited by all child classes, making bug fixing also much simpler.

FOCUS ON: NEVER DO IT TWICE

One of the most important attitudes to develop, as a programmer, is a distaste for writing the same code twice. Whenever you find yourself repeating chunks of code, it should send a shiver down your spine – this is your warning that you should find a better way of doing it. For example, could you spin the code out into a function? This is marginally more hassle the first time you do it but pays dividends once you're able to use that function the second, third and fourth time.

In fact, much programming takes this organic form. You spot an inefficiency in your code and tidy it up by creating a function. Let's say, for example, that you find yourself asking the operating system to provide the current time repeatedly. This takes several lines of code because you want it returned in a specific way. You decide this would be better in a function so you create one. Later, you find yourself doing a similar thing for the date or, perhaps, implementing a countdown timer. You create functions for each and then realise they could be organised together into a separate module called time_lib. This is great, but then you realise that you need to have multiple countdowns running at once so you finally decide to take that particular function and turn it into a class.

A Simple Class

Main.py

Let's have a look at how we can revise our circle drawing program to use object oriented principles.

http://scrib.me/1EhjumF

main.py

```
1    import pygame,circle
2    pygame.init()
3    clock = pygame.time.Clock() # Clock to limit speed
4    WIDTH=600; HEIGHT=600; BLACK=(0,0,0)
5    screen = pygame.display.set_mode([WIDTH, HEIGHT])
6    BLACK=(0,0,0)
7    screen.fill(BLACK)
8    circles=[]
9
10   for n in range(100):
11       clock.tick(25)
12       circles.append(circle.Circle(screen,WIDTH,HEIGHT))
13       pygame.display.update()
14
15   clock.tick(1)
16
17   for c in circles:
18       clock.tick(45)
19       c.clear_circle(screen)
20       pygame.display.update()
21
22   raw_input("Press a key")
```

circle.py

```
1    import pygame,random
2
3    class Circle:
4        _minimum=100; _maximum=255
5        _colour=None
6        _properties=[]
7
8        def __init__(self,screen,width,height):
9            self.random_colour()
10           self.draw_circle(screen,width,height)
11
12       def draw_circle(self,screen,width,height):
13           x=random.randint(1,width)
14           y=random.randint(1,height)
15           size=random.randint(1,5)
16           self._properties=[x,y,size]
17           pygame.draw.circle(screen,self._colour,(x,y),size)
18
19       def random_colour(self):
20           red=random.randint(self._minimum,self._maximum)
21           green=random.randint(self._minimum,self._maximum)
22           blue=random.randint(self._minimum,self._maximum)
23           self._colour=[red,green,blue]
24
25       def clear_circle(self,screen):
26           pygame.draw.circle(screen,(0,0,0),(self._properties
             [0],self._properties[1]),self._properties[2])
27
```

In the main, what we've done is to replace our *display* module with a class called *circle*. This in itself demonstrates object oriented thinking – rather than have a module draw circles over the screen, we are going to have *each circle draw itself*, so that's why we name the class this way.

You'll see immediately that two of the functions of the display module are present, largely unchanged, in our class. We begin with the keyword *class* which is used to define the block containing all the code relating to that class. You can see that every line within the block is indented – again this is how Python knows it belongs to the block.

Creating a class makes a special type of function available which is always called __init__ (with two underscores either side of the name) which is short for "initialise" and, as you might imagine, is run when the object is first created (instantiated). In this case, the __init__ function automatically runs the two functions we created for the display module – in other words, as soon as it is created our circle is drawn. This isn't always the case – the __init__ function is often used to set up the object ready for use.

You'll notice that the main difference in the code is the addition of the *self* keyword – this is critical to understanding how objects work. As you'd expect, *self* refers to the specific circle object being created at that moment. Remember the loop that runs 100 times in our main module? Each time it runs, it'll create a new object, each of which has its own *self* in exactly the same way that if you met 100 children, you might struggle to tell them apart but each would themselves know who they were – in a way it's like a personal name. So, each function has a *self* parameter to keep internal track of this.

Finally the other main change is that a new function called *clear_circle* has been created – guess what that does! We've added a new variable to the object called *_properties* (note, it's a convention to use the underscore before the names of class variables but it's not compulsory) into which we save the x and y coordinates of this particular circle, along with its size.

Now go back to our main module. Firstly, we replace *display* in the *import* statement with *circle*. You'll see that we've moved the initial setup code back here because it doesn't make sense for it to be within the *Circle* object. We also create an empty list called *circles*. Our main loop has become even simpler and line 12 is the crucial one. Just as with the *display* module, if we want to refer to a function within an imported class we must start with the name of the import – circle – followed by a full-stop followed by the name of the function. In this case, because we're creating a new object, we simply refer to it. By convention, class names start with a capital letter and our class name is *Circle* so that gets us to *circle.Circle*. This will run our __init__ function and this requires three parameters - *screen*, *WIDTH* and *HEIGHT*- so now we have *circle.Circle(screen,WIDTH,HEIGHT)*. Finally, so that we can use our objects later, we load them into a list using the append method – this simply adds one to the end. We'll end up with a list 100 objects long.

So the effect of line 12 is to create a new object based on the *Circle* class (which results in a circle being drawn on the screen) and to add that object to a list. If we were just showing the circles, then the list wouldn't be needed but, as you can see in the second for..in loop, we want to erase them also.

Line 17, then, says "for every circle in the list", line 18 sets the speed and then line 19 calls the *clear_circle* function in the class. So, it'll pull out each circle object, beginning with the first and, because each circle knows where it was painted on the screen and how big it was, we can use this self-awareness to paint a black circle on top, effectively erasing it. The old-school way of doing this would have been to keep track of this within the main program – this is fine, though not as neat, for a simple program like this but the more sophisticated a class is, the more useful it is to have it look after itself. It also makes it possible to very easily reuse it elsewhere since it's fully self-contained.

Run the program (always run the main module, not the class) and you should see the random field of circles appear, pause for a moment, and then just as sedately disappear in reverse order.

This program has been an exercise rather than a functional application – for example there's no user input at all. However, by adding input it could be turned into something more useful. For example, imagine if you painted circles across the whole screen and then paused the program. If you noted the position of the mouse pointer, you would be able to tell when it moved and respond by removing the circles using the code from line 17. What would you have? A simple screensaver – in less than 50 lines.

Again, don't worry if OOP hasn't fully sunk in – the aim of this introduction is to start you thinking in an object oriented way. The good news is that you're now equipped with all the main concepts you need to build a career, or simply personal expertise, in programming. The rest of this book will help firm up what you've learned and show you how it works in practice as we create a working game.

Extending Python

We've already seen that Python has a number of built-in functions – for example those that handle strings, lists and dictionaries – as well as a range of modules that are supplied with the language but must be imported before being used – those for random numbers and time, for example. However, part of Python's great versatility comes from the huge library of third-party modules, almost all of which are free to use. These range from very popular mainstream libraries, such as *Pygame*, to those aimed at niche uses, such as connecting a Raspberry Pi to a robot.

Let's take a quick look at some of the most important modules – especially those we're going to use in our game and project.

Pygame

Don't be fooled by the name, Pygame does much more than help you develop games – it's one of the most generally useful libraries available for Python. Remember our simple clock widget – the first thing we coded to test our setup was working? We used Pygame functions to display the window and to render the text in a nice form – indeed, most of the examples throughout this book have used Pygame even though we haven't yet started coding our game.

Pygame adds this functionality to Python:

Display – creating windows of our chosen dimensions, or allowing games and projects to run full-screen

Draw – Pygame adds a whole array of drawing options to Python including the main primitive shapes: rectangles, polygons, lines, ellipses, circles and arcs - any enclosed shape can be drawn filled or unfilled.

Surface – draws objects (such as the circles in the previous chapter) in the computer's memory so you can paint them to the display in one go – essential for games with lots of graphics

Font – embed fonts into your project then display them without relying on the end user having the same font

Image, Transform – a wide range of image manipulation functions. Indeed, Pygame has been used to create a number of specialised picture processing applications

Sprite – want to handle dozens of space invaders at once? Pygame's Sprite object allows you to create self-aware sprites with built-in collision detection, making complex games much simpler to create

Mixer, Music, Movie – Pygame makes it easy to add sounds and videos to your projects

Event – You can "listen" for all sorts of actions your players might take, most commonly key presses or mouse movements, and then run code to respond to those actions.

Pygame is written mainly in C so it's very fast (remember that one of Python's strengths is its ability to use properly prepared C libraries), something that's essential for good performance in games. It's also very portable – using Pygame you can create games and apps for every mainstream desktop operating system and a few not-so-common!

Saving Data

Whether you want to allow users to save their position within a game, store and retrieve records to a database or exchange information with a web server, you'll need to be able to read and write data. Python offers a whole range of methods for achieving this but the main ones, in order of increasing complexity are: the File object, pickle and sqlite3.

File

The File object allows you to create, save to, read from and delete simple text files. Anything you save is converted to text so, essentially, you're reading and writing strings. However, that doesn't mean you can't use File to handle pretty sophisticated data.

Let's take a very simple example to illustrate how this works. Type this listing into Geany and save it:

http://scrib.me/1wltaGp

```
1   first_name=raw_input('Type your first name...')
2   second_name=raw_input('Type your surname...')
3   savefile=open('data.dat','w')
4   savefile.write(first_name+'\n')
5   savefile.write(second_name+'\n')
6   savefile.close()
7   print('Saved')
8   first_name=None
9   second_name=None
10  openfile=open('data.dat','r')
11  name=openfile.read().split()
12  first_name=name[0]
13  second_name=name[1]
14  print first_name+" "+second_name
15
```

I'm sure you'll immediately spot that the purpose of the first two lines is to get the user to type in their first and second names. The interesting stuff begins on line 3 where we create a new variable using the file object's *open* method (remember, functions are called methods when inside objects). We pass in the name of the text file – this can be any name we choose as long as it's valid for our operating system (if the file doesn't already exist, it will be created by Python at this point). The 'w' parameter means that we want to write to the file – in other words we want to save some data. In line 4 we write the first name – by appending "\n" we add a new line. This is the file equivalent of pressing the enter key – essentially we're using file to organise text by line so by inserting a \n at this point the surname will appear separately a line below. You could also simply add a delimiter to each saved record – the pipe symbol | for example – but you must choose a character that you would never use within a record.

Having written the second name to the file we then close it – this tells the operating system to save the file with its new contents.

We're now going to open it up again and read the contents back in. Lines 9 and 10 clear the name variables so we can be sure we've read in the file and not simply kept what the user typed. On line 10 we create a new file object, using the same name but this time the parameter 'r' which reads in the contents of a file but leaves it unchanged. Since files only contain text, *openfile* is a string at the moment which means we can use the *split()* function to take this text and create from it a list with each of the lines as a separate element.

For example, if the user's name was Joe Bloggs, printing *name* would result in:

['Joe','Bloggs']

So, to retrieve the first name we use *name[0]* and for the surname we use *name[1]*. Run the program and you should see your name reappear in the terminal. There's an even better test, however – go to data.dat (if you've used the same name) and open it in a text editor. You should see the names there, one per line.

The file object is the workhorse of Python file input/output and, as you can see, it's pretty simple to use.

Pickle

The great benefit of *pickle* is that, unlike *file*, it can take any data form and save it to a file. It can also "unpickle" the data back to exactly its original form. In fact, pickle is specifically built to augment the built-in file object and make it more useful.

Again, this is best understood through a short example:

http://scrib.me/1J1uxkF

```
1  import pickle
2  save_data={'username':'Joe Bloggs','score':9234
   ,'max_level':5}
3  save_file=open("savedata.dat",'wb')
4  pickle.dump(save_data,save_file)
5  save_file.close()
6  #zero variables, read file back in
7  progress_file=open("savedata.dat",'rb')
8  progress_data=pickle.load(progress_file)
9  print "Dear "+progress_data['username']+",
   your data \n"+str(progress_data)
```

Note that we must begin with an *import* statement – pickle is part of the standard Python install but, because it's not quite as basic an object as *file*, it must be explicitly added to the code. You don't have to install it, however, if you're using Windows, Mac or Linux (including Raspbian)

On line 2 we create a dictionary containing some basic data including the user's name, their current score and the furthest they've reached in our imaginary game. Next, we create a file object with the parameter 'wb' which stands for "write bytes". This is because pickle uses the file object to save its data but, rather than saving it as text, it uses its own format to convert the information. By using 'wb', it's able to use a much larger set of characters to achieve this, but the end result would look like gobbledygook if you opened it in a text editor.

Line 4 uses the attractively named pickle.dump method to save the data – passing it the data itself (it could be just about any variable type, we're using a dictionary) and the file object. We then close the file.

In a real game, you'd probably want to read this data back in later or, indeed, in a later game session and the code from line 7 achieves this. We create a new file object – this time with the 'rb' parameter because we're reading bytes back in. On line 8, we create a new variable and use it to receive the data from pickle using the load method. Line 9 prints it out.

Pickle is a very powerful and widely used module. Its main advantage over the simpler file object is that you don't need to write code to parse (read and convert) the saved data when you want to retrieve it - pickle simply gives it back to you in the same format you used to save it. If you think about the amount of information you're likely to want to save in your game (a leaderboard, for example) you can appreciate how much simpler pickle makes this – not only saving time but reducing the chances of bugs creeping in.

SQLite3

If you get into commercial programming then you'll encounter SQL (Structured Query Language and no, it is NOT pronounced "Sequel") pretty quickly. Pickle is excellent for storing relatively small amounts of unstructured data but if you wanted to create a customer database or to store huge amounts of information for a football league manager game, for example, you need something more capable.

The main advantage of relational databases (the sort of databases SQL is most often used with) is that they make the retrieving of data lightning quick. After all, if you have a large database of Conference League footballers and you want to list all players for sale, this needs to happen in the blink of an eye to avoid your game appearing slow.

SQLite is a half-way house between the ease of use and versatility of pickle and the full-fat power and complexity of, for example, MySQL (the database format used by a large percentage of websites). It's a cross-platform standard and represents data in a flat form similar, in concept, to card indexes. It isn't good at cross-indexing data but it's very good at simple retrieval – for example it'd make mincemeat of our "players for sale" query.

Python's SQLite3 module allows you to create, edit, read and write SQLite files and, if you intend to find work as a programmer, it's a good place to start learning about SQL whilst also being very useful. SQL itself is standard across its many forms so your experience of SQLite3 with Python would give you a head start when faced with learning any other mainstream database.

To do things with SQL databases, you write queries and then execute those queries using your chosen SQL engine. So, our Conference League player search might look something like this:

```
SELECT * FROM players WHERE league = 'conf' AND status = 'for sale'
```

It really is that straightforward – but as this isn't a book about SQL I'll move along. The key point to bear in mind is that it's nothing to be frightened of, you can carry out most database functions with a small range of commonly used techniques.

Congratulations

So far in this book you've seen how to set up your environment, how programs work and how to think like a programmer. You've had a whistle-stop tour of the basics of Python programming so you now know the most useful variable types; how to create and use functions, modules and objects and how to structure your code using decisions and loops. In this section, you've learned about the extra functionality Pygame adds, as well as the various ways to store and retrieve data using Python modules.

The best way to reinforce your knowledge and make sure it sticks is to put it into practice so I'm going to cover, in great detail, the development of two very different projects. You've learned a lot so far but don't expect to remember everything – even the most experienced programmers consider Google to be their best friend. Programming is much more about technique and knowing which tool from the toolkit to use in each situation than it is about remembering the specifics of how Python, or any other language, implements that tool. Once you've completed the projects, you should have a very good idea of which situations call for a loop, which require a decision and when it's best to spin out your functions into separate objects. This only comes through practice so it's time to roll up your sleeves and get stuck in.

Part 4

CREATING A SIMPLE GAME

Design

In this section we're going to design and create a simple game. By doing this, not only will we create an end-product that will be fun to play but we'll also explore many of the programming skills you'll use for more general projects.

To get the most out of this section, it's really important that you type in the exercises as we go through. This way, you'll better understand what each line and statement does within the game. All the resources can be found here: http://www.rpilab.net/code/code-for-part-4-designing-a-game/ (shortcode : http://scrib.me/rpis4code). I suggest downloading the ZIP file from that location onto your computer (Raspberry Pi, PC or Mac) and extracting it.

Alternatively, you can see each snippet of code by using the QR codes embedded in the following section.

Designing a game

However simple the game, you shouldn't just sit down at your computer and start coding away - that will result in nothing but chaos and frustration. You need to begin by thinking carefully about exactly how your game is going to work and, from that, generate a list of the tasks both you and your code will need to complete.

FOCUS ON: SPECIFICATIONS

If you follow a career in programming, you'll quickly come across the concept of the "specification". This is a document that is created before programming starts and fully details what the application does, how it works and what it looks like. Different programming teams use different specifications and many now adopt a more rapid development approach called "agile" which minimises the up-front work and focuses more on smaller work units that evolve as the project progresses. For a simple game, our specification will be brief.

Genres of games

According to Wikipedia (en.wikipedia.org/wiki/Video_game_genres) there are 13 major genres including action, role-playing, strategy, sports and puzzle. One way to come up with game ideas is to look through the genres and think about examples from each. By doing this, you expose yourself to lots of different concepts and you'll probably be inspired. The other option is to play plenty of games - whether that's on a phone, console or computer - and think about what you enjoy the most.

Having said that, don't bite off more than you can chew - a space invaders clone is achievable by a new programmer working on their own whereas a first person shooter inspired by Call of Duty is not.

The Concept

In this case, we're going to choose a simple shoot 'em up which we're going to call Pi Splat. We're using the Raspberry Pi as our inspiration so, naturally, our targets are going to be fruit. The concept can be summarised like this:

We're being invaded! Several types of fruit fall from the top of the screen but beware - most types are poisonous. Your job is to use a mobile gun platform to destroy the poisonous fruit, but to allow only the raspberries through to reach the ground. When enough raspberries have landed, the planetary defences will be activated and the population will be saved.

Okay, it's not exactly the most original concept but it's simple and fun - two excellent traits for our first game.

But what, exactly, is a game? To qualify, a program must have two things: clearly defined, consistent rules and a "victory condition". Let's look at those in turn.

Rules

In real life there's nothing to stop you creating your own card game and making up the rules as you play at the kitchen table. You can't do this with video games - the computer cannot improvise, it needs to know what to do in every conceivable situation.

In the case of our game, the rules are very simple:

1. Fruit appears randomly and drops vertically down the screen, disappearing if it reaches the bottom

2. The gun turret can be moved left and right along the bottom of the screen. Pressing the Fire button launches a bullet up the screen

3. If a bullet collides with a fruit, the fruit is destroyed

4. If the destroyed fruit is not a raspberry, the player receives points

5. If the destroyed fruit is a raspberry, the player loses points

6. If a raspberry reaches the bottom of the screen, the player receives points

7. If any other fruit reaches the bottom of the screen, the player loses points

8. Once a pre-determined number of raspberries have reached the bottom, the level ends

9. As levels pass, the speed of the falling fruit increases.

Victory Condition

For an app to be a game, as opposed to some other leisure activity, it must have an aim - on achieving that aim, the player is said to have won. In fact, in games that have multiple levels, there is often one victory condition for the levels and a different, overall, aim for the game as a whole.

In the case of Angry Birds, for example, the aim of each level is to destroy all the pigs on the screen. The victory condition of the game as whole, on the other hand, is to complete all the levels.

For our game, the aim of each level is to collect the prescribed number of raspberries - the aim of the game as a whole is to clear 5 levels.

Look and feel

We'll design the game by using the principles of Input, Logic and Output. So, what sort of input do you think a game like this would have?

Input

Firstly, the user needs to control the gun. This means we'll have to set up a way for the player to use their keyboard or mouse to move left and right, as well as firing. In this case we're going to stick with keyboard control as it works better for a game of this sort, so we need to write code to specify which keys the player can use to control their gun turret and more code to "listen" for those key presses.

We'll also want the user to be able to save their progress so they can exit the game and resume later. So, when the game loads, it needs to check whether there's any progress data and, if so, read it as an input.

Output

The game's graphics are the most obvious form of output. We'll need to create images for each of the fruits and write code to handle their motion down the screen. To dress it up a little, we'll also add an explosion effect when the fruits are hit. To help with the player's input, we must create a turret graphic and bullets. Finally, we'll need to generate the screen decoration for the background, game instructions, score reports and so forth.

We can use this to build a list of the graphics we'll need:

Fruit: raspberry, cherry, strawberry, pear and banana

Player graphics: turret and bullets

Background graphic

Splash screen

Sound is also a form of output so we might want to include:

In-game music

Special effects

We will also be saving the player's progress data as a form of output.

Logic
Our logic code will check whether bullets have collided with fruits and update the score accordingly. It will also keep track of which level is being played and when the game is over.

Where to find graphics and sounds
If you're an artist or musician, you can, of course, create your own graphics or sounds. However, if you don't have those talents you can either commission someone to create them or use online libraries. If you opt for a library, then you must carefully check what you are allowed to do with any resources you download - especially if you intend to edit them.

You can find free graphics at openclipart.org - in the vast majority of cases you can freely amend these resources and use them as you wish.

en.fotolia.com is an excellent source of top quality graphics and photos for a small cost. For most purposes, you should download the vector format of the image and edit it in Inkscape (www.inkscape.org), DrawPlus (http://www.serif.com/free-graphic-design-software/) or Adobe Illustrator.

The best source of free sounds is freesound.org - you'll find everything from music loops to special effects.

Creating the basic game

Programming is about writing code, so the sooner you get to open up your editor and start typing the better. Creating a simple game, however, is a completely different process to building a real world object such as a house. In that case you need to have a detailed blueprint before you dig the first hole. Programming, in contrast, is more like building a house out of Lego - you select from a tool-set of pre-created blocks and build one part at a time, experimenting and amending along the way. It's an iterative and organic process in which you focus on the building blocks of the program - writing, testing and editing code to create each function, module and class - before bringing them together to make the final product.

You can find the code, images and other resources for this game at *http://scrib.me/rpis4code. www.pygame.org/docs* contains specific information about pygame functions and the documentation for Python 2.7 is at *http://docs.python.org/2/index.html*

Important: I'm *not* going to go into detail about every single command used in this code. You've met much of it earlier in this book but where a command or function is new we will explain what it does but we expect you to use the documentation for Python and pygame to learn the detail. Not only does this keep the pace fast and the book to a manageable length, but it encourages one of the main skills any modern day programmer needs: the ability to use the documentation.

You'll also notice our code doesn't include many programming comments (text following the # symbol that describes what the code does). This is also to make the code as clean and short as possible. The downloadable code (which you should look through after completing the chapter) is heavily documented.

We're going to begin by creating a simple template for our game - it'll then be a case of filling out the template to get the game working. To create the template, we need to think about how our code will be organised in terms of graphics, sounds and Python files - and we do this using the familiar structure of input, logic and output from the previous chapter. Broadly speaking you should expect to create a class for each of the game's visible objects. You could add the code for each of these classes in the main Python file but it makes more sense to have each in its own file - not only is this clearer and easier to understand but it also removes clutter from the main program code.

http://scrib.me/pi_splat_1

1: main.py

Create a folder to contain your Python game. Now, in Geany, create and save a file called main.py. Type the code in listing 1 (overleaf) and save.

2: classes

```
1   class Bullet():
2       def __init__(self):
3           pass
4
```

Create Python files with the following names: *bullet.py*, *fruit.py*, *turret.py* and *game.py*. You can see the bullet class here - all the others are exactly the same format, simply replace *Bullet* with the name of the class in each one.

The first three are straight out of our design document and represent visible objects. The game class is different - it's there to hold information about the game as a whole. For example, it makes sense to keep track of the player's score and level number and, whilst you can do this using separate variables, by storing the information within a game object you make it clear what the purpose of each variable is. You can also reuse it across multiple projects

Remember, you can see the code at http://scrib.me/pi_splat_1

3: images

Create a subfolder called "images" and copy the game's graphic files into it. You can get these from *http://scrib.me/rpis4code* - choose the "initial files" option.

FOCUS ON: PICTURE AND SOUND FORMATS

The images used in this game are saved in .png format. This is because PNGs can have a transparent background - if you used .jpg, for example, you'd see a white edge to each of the fruits. When developing games for the Raspberry Pi, you need to choose the most efficient format for each graphic and for those with transparent backgrounds the 8-bit PNG format with alpha transparency works well. As you'll remember, an 8-bit image can only include a maximum of 256 colours (a 32 bit PNG can contain millions of colours) which gives the Pi less work to do when it's painting each screen. For most purposes, then, this is the format to use.

With short sounds (for example those used for special effects), .wav is a good format as, although the file size is larger, the computer doesn't have to decompress it. For longer sounds that are loaded once at the start of the game - background music for example - mp3 is a better choice

---

Boilerplate: main.py

```
1   import math, random, pygame, sys
2   from fruit import *; from game import *; from turret
    import *; from bullet import *
3
4   ##TOP LEVEL CONSTANTS
5   FPS = 30
6   WINDOWWIDTH=480; WINDOWHEIGHT=640
7   GAMETITLE="Pi Splat"
8   WHITE=[255,255,255]; RED=[255,0,0]; GREEN=[0,255,0];
    BLUE=[0,0,255]; BLACK=[0,0,0]
9
10
11  def main():
12      #set up initial display
13      pygame.init()
14      clock=pygame.time.Clock()
15      surface=pygame.display.set_mode([WINDOWWIDTH,
        WINDOWHEIGHT])
16      pygame.display.set_caption(GAMETITLE)
17
18      #MAIN GAME LOOP
19      game_over=False
20
21      while game_over==False:
22          for event in pygame.event.get():
23              if event.type==pygame.KEYDOWN:
24                  if event.key==pygame.K_ESCAPE:
25                      game_over=True
26          print pygame.time.get_ticks()
27          pygame.display.update()
28          clock.tick(FPS)
29
30  if __name__ == '__main__':
31      main()
32
```

Listing 1

The initial 30 lines of our program comprise the "boilerplate" or standard structure that hardly varies from game to game. Line 2 imports our classes. We then set a series of constants - variables whose values will not change during the game. Unlike many other languages, Python doesn't have a separate type for constants so we name them using capital letters so we can identify them later.

On line 10 we set up a function called *main* which is where our program will begin. Lines 12-15 use pygame functions to draw the initial window for the game. Lines 20 to 27 constitute the *main loop* - this is the code used to draw the screen many times per second as the game is being played.

We set up a variable called *game_over* in line 18 and give it the value *False*. We then start a *while* loop which will keep repeating until *game_over* becomes *True*. The *for* loop at line 21 asks pygame if any events have taken place. In this case, we're interested in keyboard events so, in line 22, we cycle through all the events in the queue and, if a key has been pressed, we then ask if that key was Esc. If it was, we set *game_over* to *True*, causing the game to exit.

Line 26 updates the display (although we haven't yet added anything visual - we will do soon) and line 27 tells pygame to make sure the loop doesn't cycle more quickly than 30 times per second. Finally, lines 29 and 30 are used to make sure that the main function will only be accessed if this was the file open in Geany when we clicked the cog button. In other words, if we accidentally imported this module into another, *main* would not be called.

Now click the cog (or press F5). You should see a series of numbers running down the terminal window - these are generated by line 25 and are simply the number of milliseconds since the program started, proving that you've typed everything correctly and are ready to move on. If you see any error messages in the terminal window, you need to correct them before continuing.

Let there be fruit

We're going to begin by making the fruit appear and drop down the screen. Naturally, we'll start by setting up the fruit object. Open up fruit.py in Geany and type in the new code:

http://scrib.me/pi_splat_2

```
1    import pygame, random
2    class Fruit(pygame.sprite.Sprite):
3
4        def __init__(self,WINDOWWIDTH):
5            pygame.sprite.Sprite.__init__(self)
6            self._species=random.choice(["raspberry",
                 "strawberry","cherry","pear","banana"])
7            self.image=pygame.image.load("images/"+self.
                 _species+".png")
8            self.rect=self.image.get_rect()
9            self.rect.y=0-self.rect.height
10           self.rect.x=(random.randint(self.rect.width/2,(
                 WINDOWWIDTH-self.rect.width)))
11
12       def update_position(self,level,WINDOWHEIGHT,game):
13           if self.rect.y<(WINDOWHEIGHT):
14               self.rect.y+=2+level
15           else:
16               if self._species=="raspberry":
17                   game.update_score(50)
18                   game.update_raspberries_saved()
19               else:
20                   game.update_score(-10)
21               self.kill()
22
23       def shot(self,game):
24           if self._species=="raspberry":
25               game.update_score(-50)
26           else:
27               game.update_score(10)
28           self.kill()
```

We begin by importing the pygame library and the *random* module. Take a look at line 2 - you can see that we've added *pygame.sprite.Sprite* to the class definition. This is class inheritance in action - this line tells Python to create a new object based on pygame's *Sprite* class. In other words Python is to assume that this object is a sprite unless we tell it otherwise. A sprite is a specialised object based on an image and it contains all the functions needed to handle the visual side of our fruit.

The __init__ function is run when the main program creates a new instance of the *Fruit* class - in other words when we want a new fruit to appear and fall down the screen. In line 6 we create a property of the sprite which we've named *_species* - in fact it's just a variable like any other but the convention is to call variables that are inside objects "properties". The *self* keyword in front of a variable name tells the object that this variable is part of its unique identity and should be remembered. So every Fruit instance will remember which species it was set to for as long as it's alive - this is a very useful feature of objects as we'll see.

In line 7 we use pygame's *image* functions to load a picture into the sprite. The next line makes sure that the size of the sprite matches the size of the image just loaded. Line 9 sets the y (vertical) position to zero minus the height of the image. So if the picture was 50 pixels tall, the top left corner of the fruit will be drawn at -50 so it's just off the top of the screen. Line 10 is a little more complicated but you can see that we want the horizontal (x) position of the fruit to be randomised. *Random.randint* takes two parameters which set the range between which you want it to generate a number. The first parameter, in this case is :

```
self.rect.width/2
```

In other words, the lowest horizontal value is to be half the width of the image from the left - this ensures the fruit is never drawn either wholly or partially off the left edge of the screen. The other parameter is:

```
WINDOWWIDTH-self.rect.width
```

In this case, the maximum right hand position will be the width of the window minus the width of the image. So with a WINDOWWIDTH of 480 pixels and a fruit width of, say, 72 pixels we'd be asking *Random.randint* to provide a random number between 36 (72/2) and 408 (480-72). That number would be used to position the fruit - each one in a different horizontal location.

FOCUS ON: WHY USE VARIABLES FOR CONSTANTS?

Why bother with WINDOWWIDTH given that it's the same throughout our game (otherwise it wouldn't be a constant), why not just use 480? Firstly because this allows you to create a new game with a different width by doing nothing more than changing the value once at the start of the program rather than altering every occurrence of 480. The second reason is that it makes reading your code much simpler - by using WINDOWWIDTH rather than 480 in a calculation, you know exactly what that number represents.

The _init_ function, then, sets things up but we need to add more functions to make things happen. These functions will vary depending on the purpose of the class and in this case the most obvious attribute of our fruit is that it moves down the screen so we'll begin with a function called *update_position*. Unlike _init_, this function will only run when it's called (in this case by the main program).

The function definition in line 12 includes 4 parameters that must be passed to it. *Self* is part of all class definitions but the others are our own variables. *WINDOWHEIGHT* is self-explanatory, *game* is the game object (we haven't created it yet) and *speed* is a parameter we'll set in main.py shortly.

The function is pretty simple. On line 13 we check to see if the vertical position of the fruit is still less than the height of the window (if it isn't, then the fruit must have dropped off the bottom). If it is, then in line 14 we increase its y position by an amount related to the speed.

If the fruit has dropped out of the window then Python will execute the code after the *else* in line 15. In this case, the code is another *if* statement - it's very important to understand that the code between lines 16 and 20 will only be executed *if line 13 is false*.

So, on line 16 we check to see if the current fruit is a raspberry. Remember that the point of the game is to allow raspberries to pass through so, in that case, we are going to increase the score and increment the number of raspberries saved so far (the game ends when this number gets to 10). Note that we haven't added any code to the *game* object yet but we now know which functions to create.

Line 19 translates as "if the fruit is not on-screen (because it's reached the bottom) and it's not a raspberry then execute the next line" - in this case line 20 decreases the score because the player has allowed one of the other fruits to reach the bottom. Finally, line 22 deletes the object- why? Look at the indentation - line 22 gets executed if the fruit has reached the bottom but it is not inside the *if* structure starting on line 16 so the object will be "killed" whichever fruit type it is. This makes sense - once the fruit has disappeared, we want to clear it and stop it updating otherwise it'll continue to fall even though we can't see it.

Finally, we add a function called *shot* since the object of the game is to destroy fruit other than raspberries. Go through each line and work out what's happening - it's pretty straightforward.

Setting up the game

Note: refer to http://scrib.me/pi_splat_2 for these files

game.py

```
 1  class Game():
 2      def __init__(self):
 3          self._score=0
 4          self._raspberries_saved=0
 5
 6      def update_score(self,amount):
 7          self._score+=amount
 8
 9      def get_score(self):
10          return self._score
11
12      def update_raspberries_saved(self):
13          self._raspberries_saved+=1
14
15      def get_raspberries_saved(self):
16          return self._raspberries_saved
```

By writing our *Fruit* class, we already know what we need (initially at least) in our *Game* class. Remember that the *Game* class is different to *Fruit* because it isn't visible - it's just a convenient wrapper for code and variables that relate to the game as a whole.

The class definition doesn't contain anything between the brackets because we're not basing *Game* on a pre-existing class. The __init__ function initialises two variables - the score and the number of raspberries we've saved - so we can use them later. *update_score* takes the amount sent to it and adds that to the running score (see line 17 of fruit.py to see this function called). *get_score*, on the other hand, uses the *return* keyword to send back the score. The final two functions fulfil the same purpose for the *raspberries_saved* variable.

Updating main.py

We've now filled out our boilerplate a little. Firstly, we've added a new constant called *SPEED* at line 9. The next change is at line 22 where we create a sprite group - this is essentially a list of all the fruit sprites so we can easily handle them later. The *if* statement beginning at line

```
1    import math,random,pygame,sys,pickle,os
2    from fruit import *; from game import *; from turret
     import *; from bullet import *
3
4    ##TOP LEVEL CONSTANTS
5    FPS = 30
6    WINDOWWIDTH=480; WINDOWHEIGHT=640
7    GAMETITLE="Pi Splat"
8    WHITE=[255,255,255]; RED=[255,0,0]; GREEN=[0,255,0];
     BLUE=[0,0,255]; BLACK=[0,0,0]
9    SPEED=0.5
10
11   def main():
12       game=Game()
13
14       #set up initial display
15       pygame.init()
16       clock=pygame.time.Clock()
17       surface=pygame.display.set_mode([WINDOWWIDTH,
         WINDOWHEIGHT])
18       pygame.display.set_caption(GAMETITLE)
19
```

```
20        #MAIN GAME LOOP
21        game_over=False
22        live_fruit_sprites=pygame.sprite.Group()
23        ticktock=1
24        while game_over==False:
25            for event in pygame.event.get():
26                if event.type==pygame.KEYDOWN:
27                    if event.key==pygame.K_ESCAPE:
28                        game_over=True
29
30            if ticktock % (FPS/SPEED)==1:
31                if len(live_fruit_sprites)<10:
32                    live_fruit_sprites.add((Fruit(
                          WINDOWWIDTH)))
33
34            surface.fill(BLACK)
35            for sprite in live_fruit_sprites:
36                sprite.update_position(SPEED,WINDOWHEIGHT,
                      game)
37
38            live_fruit_sprites.draw(surface)
39
40            pygame.display.update()
41
42            ticktock+=1
43
44            clock.tick(FPS)
45
46  if __name__ == '__main__':
47      main()
```

31 creates a new fruit object and adds it to the sprite group if there are fewer than 10 fruit objects on-screen. You'll notice we created a variable called *ticktock* on line 23 and we use it on line 30. This is needed because the main loop (beginning at line 24) runs at 30 frames per second (see line 45) so, without the code at line 30, all the fruits would be added almost instantaneously rather than spread out. You can see from line 43 that ticktock increments each loop, so it'll be worth 30 after a second, 60 after two seconds and so on. Line 30 says that if you divide *ticktock* by the result of frames per second (30 in this case) divided by the speed variable (0.5 at the moment) and get a remainder of 1 (that's what the % or modulus means), run line 31 and add a fruit if there are fewer than 10.

Yes, it's a bit of a brain-melter but here's an example which should make it clearer. Let's say *ticktock* is worth 60 (after 2 seconds or so). (FPS/SPEED) will always be 30/0.5 which gives 60 so the equation becomes what is the remainder of 60/60? The answer is zero (60 goes into 60 exactly once with no remainder). However, in the next game loop cycle, ticktock will be worth 61 so, this time, there will be a remainder of 1 and so a fruit can be added.

If you think it through, you'll see that the next time there will be a remainder of 1 is when ticktock is worth 121 (after 4 seconds). The effect, then, is to run line 32 every two seconds or so which is exactly what we want. Why not simply use Python's time functions? You could - but then if the computer is struggling with the frame rate (as might be the case with the Raspberry Pi), the fruit could end up being added more slowly than intended.

Line 34 fills the window with black (you'll be able to see what happens if you don't do this in a moment). Line 36 cycles through every fruit (if there are any) and, in line 37, runs the Fruit class's *update_position* function we just created - moving each one down the screen or deleting it. Finally, on line 39 we run pygame's *draw* function which will paint every fruit to the screen in one go.

Now it's time to give it a try. Make sure main.py is in your Geany window and press F5 or click the cog. You should see fruit appear at the top and move smoothly down the window. Close the terminal to stop the program and add a hash symbol (#) to the start of line 34 - this "comments out" the line so that Python ignores it. Press F5 and you should see a very different result.

Shooting Fruit

turret.py

We're only a few steps away from having a working game. Let's start with the gun turret.

```
1    import pygame
2    class Turret(pygame.sprite.Sprite):
3        def __init__(self,WINDOWWIDTH,WINDOWHEIGHT):
4            pygame.sprite.Sprite.__init__(self)
5            self.image=pygame.image.load("images/turret.png")
6            self.rect = self.image.get_rect()
7            self.rect.x = (WINDOWWIDTH-self.rect.width)/2
8            self.rect.y =WINDOWHEIGHT-self.rect.height
9
10       def update_position(self,direction,WINDOWWIDTH):
11           if direction=="left" and self.rect.x>10:
12               self.rect.x-=10
13           elif direction=="right" and self.rect.x<(
             WINDOWWIDTH-10):
14               self.rect.x+=10
15
16       def get_gun_position(self):
17           position={}
18           position["x"]=self.rect.x+(self.rect.width/2)
19           position["y"]=self.rect.y-(self.rect.height/2)
20           return position
```

Much of the code is the same as for the Fruit class with lines 7 and 8 positioning the turret graphic at the centre of the screen's bottom edge - see if you can decipher how the code works.

update_position is pretty self-explanatory - it takes the direction and the width of the window as parameters and then deducts from the turret's horizontal (x) position to send the graphic left or adds to it to send it right. Again, see if you can work out how the code prevents the turret graphic from disappearing off the left or right hand side of the screen.

Finally, we add a function to send back the position of the gun in the centre of the turret. This is because we're going to want to start our bullets from that position so that they look as though they're emerging from the gun.

bullet.py

```
1   import pygame
2   class Bullet(pygame.sprite.Sprite):
3       def __init__(self,position):
4           pygame.sprite.Sprite.__init__(self)
5           self.image=pygame.image.load("images/bullet.png")
6           self.rect = self.image.get_rect()
7           self.rect.x=position["x"]
8           self.rect.y=position["y"]
9
10      def update_position(self):
11
12          if self.rect.y>=-self.rect.height:
13              self.rect.y-=5
14          else:
15              self.kill()
```

The bullet class is very similar again. In the _init_ function we send the gun position from Turret. The function *update_position* is very simple but bear in mind that bullets go up the screen so their *y* value gets smaller. Once they go off the top, we destroy the sprite.

main.py

```
1   import math,random,pygame,sys
2   from fruit import *; from game import *; from turret import *; from bullet import *
3
4   ##TOP LEVEL CONSTANTS
5   FPS = 30
6   WINDOWWIDTH=480; WINDOWHEIGHT=640
7   GAMETITLE="Pi Splat"
8   WHITE=[255,255,255]; RED=[255,0,0]; GREEN=[0,255,0];
    BLUE=[0,0,255]; BLACK=[0,0,0]
9   SPEED=0.5
10
11  def main():
12      game=Game()
13
14      #set up initial display
15      pygame.init()
16      pygame.key.set_repeat(1, 75)
17      scoreFont=pygame.font.Font("256BYTES.TTF",32)
18      clock=pygame.time.Clock()
19      surface=pygame.display.set_mode([WINDOWWIDTH,
        WINDOWHEIGHT])
20      pygame.display.set_caption(GAMETITLE)
21
```

```
22    #MAIN GAME LOOP
23    game_over=False
24    live_fruit_sprites=pygame.sprite.Group()
25    bullet_sprites=pygame.sprite.Group()
26    other_sprites=pygame.sprite.Group()
27    turret=Turret(WINDOWWIDTH,WINDOWHEIGHT)
28    other_sprites.add(turret)
29    ticktock=1
30
31    while game_over==False:
32        for event in pygame.event.get():
33            if event.type==pygame.KEYDOWN:
34                if event.key==pygame.K_ESCAPE:
35                    game_over=True
36                elif event.key==pygame.K_LEFT:
37                    turret.update_position("left",WINDOWWIDTH)
38                elif event.key==pygame.K_RIGHT:
39                    turret.update_position("right",WINDOWWIDTH)
40                elif event.key==pygame.K_SPACE:
41                    bullet=Bullet(turret.get_gun_position())
42                    bullet_sprites.add(bullet)
43
44        if ticktock % (FPS/SPEED)==1:
45            if len(live_fruit_sprites)<10:
46                live_fruit_sprites.add((Fruit(WINDOWWIDTH)))
47
48        for sprite in bullet_sprites:
49            sprite.update_position()
50
51        collisions=pygame.sprite.groupcollide(live_fruit_sprites,
              bullet_sprites,False,True)
52
53        if collisions:
54            for fruit in collisions:
55                fruit.shot(game)
56
57
58        surface.fill(BLACK)
59        bullet_sprites.draw(surface)
60        other_sprites.draw(surface)
```

We need to make a few changes to main.py to tie it all together and finish the first version of the game. Line 16 is a pygame function that limits the repeat interval on a keypress to 75 milliseconds - this is to allow the player to repeatedly press their space bar to fire bullets. Line 17 imports a custom font (www.1001freefonts.com is a good place to find them) which we'll use to display the score. In lines 25 to 29, we create two new sprite groups - one to hold the bullets and a catch-all group for any other sprites we're adding. Why do we need separate groups for fruit and bullets? Wait and see...

Lines 36 to 39 respond to the left and right arrow keys and update the turret's position using the code we just added to turret.py. Lines

40 to 42 create a new bullet every time the space bar is pressed and add the bullet to the group. Lines 48 and 49 cycle through all the bullets currently visible and trigger the *update_position* function.

Line 51 is a little bit of pygame magic. In this one line, we can check whether any bullet collides with any fruit - if so, pygame generates a list of those fruits that have collided. All we do is pass in the two sprite groups we want to check (hence the need for separate groups for bullets and fruit) along with two other parameters that indicate whether pygame should immediately kill colliding sprites. In the case of the fruit sprites, we send a *False* parameter because we want to update the score before killing them manually. For the bullets, it's fine for pygame to kill them straight away. This one line replaces the dozens that would be necessary in Python if we didn't use pygame.

In lines 53 to 55 we iterate through any collisions and run the *shot* function of the fruit object the bullet has hit. Lines 59 and 60 draw the new groups to the screen.

```
61
62      for sprite in live_fruit_sprites:
63          sprite.update_position(SPEED,WINDOWHEIGHT,game)
64
65      live_fruit_sprites.draw(surface)
66
67      scoreText=scoreFont.render('Score: '+str(game.get_score
        ()),True,GREEN)
68      surface.blit(scoreText,(10,10))
69      pygame.display.update()
70
71      ticktock+=1
72      if game.get_raspberries_saved()>=10:
73          game_over=True
74
75      clock.tick(FPS)
76
77  #handle end of game
78  surface.fill(BLACK)
79  scoreText=scoreFont.render('Game over. Score: '+str(game.
    get_score()),True,GREEN)
80  surface.blit(scoreText,(10,200))
81  pygame.display.update()
82
83  raw_input("press any key")
84
85 if __name__ == '__main__':
86     main()
87
```

On line 67 we use pygame's *font.render* to create a picture that displays the score in green with a transparent background using the font we created earlier. Line 68 paints the score onto the screen using the *blit* function. You must use this function to draw objects onto the screen if you're not using sprites, otherwise they won't appear.

Lines 72 and 73 set up a simple *if* statement that breaks out of the main game loop once we've saved 10 raspberries.

Finally, the code from lines 78 to 83 clears the screen, draws the final score and waits for the user to press any key.

Once your code matches our listings, save and press F5 to play the game. Whilst it's certainly basic, you now have a fully working, playable, arcade game in less than 200 lines of code. Not bad.

Completing the Game

To turn "Pi Splat" into a working game, we need to add levels that get progressively harder. While we're at it, we need a splash/instructions screen at the start and the ability to save and restore the player's progress. We'll also smooth out a few rough edges to give the game a more professional polish.

You can download the documented code for the full game at *http://scrib.me/rpis4code*. You can either type the lines in, following along, or load the code into Geany and follow the discussion. You can see the code at this location: http://scrib.me/pi_splat_3

main.py

```
1   import math,random,pygame,sys,pickle,os
2   from fruit import *; from game import *; from turret import *; from
    bullet import *
3
4   ##TOP LEVEL CONSTANTS
5   FPS = 30
6   WINDOWWIDTH=480; WINDOWHEIGHT=640
7   GAMETITLE="Pi Splat"
8   WHITE=[255,255,255]; RED=[255,0,0]; GREEN=[0,255,0]; BLUE=[0,0,255
    ]; BLACK=[0,0,0]
9   NUMBER_OF_LEVELS=5
10
11  def main():
12      game=Game()
13
14      #INITIAL SETUP
15      pygame.init()
16      pygame.key.set_repeat(1, 75)
17      pygame.mouse.set_visible(False)
18      displayFont=pygame.font.Font("256BYTES.TTF",28)
19      clock=pygame.time.Clock()
20      surface=pygame.display.set_mode([WINDOWWIDTH,WINDOWHEIGHT])
21      pygame.display.set_caption(GAMETITLE)
22
23      #SPLASH SCREEN
24      splash=pygame.image.load("images/splash.png")
25      surface.blit(splash,(0,0))
26      pygame.display.update()
27      game_over=False
28      start_game=False
29
```

Most of the work will take place in main.py. This makes sense because adding levels, for example, involves changing the structure of the program much more than changing how individual objects such as fruits or bullets behave.

On line 1, we add two new modules: *pickle* and *os*. Both of these are needed so that we can save the user's progress. We remove the *SCORE* constant and replace it with *NUMBER_OF_LEVELS* which we're setting to 5. You could increase or decrease the number of levels in your version of the game by altering this number.

At line 23 we've added some code to create a splash screen. The screen itself has been created as a single graphic - it might have been more flexible to add the text at runtime but a static image is fine for a simple game like this.

At line 24, we load the splash screen and then *blit* it to the surface on line 25 before refreshing the screen on the next line so that it becomes visible. We've moved the *game_over* variable to this point because the user needs to be able to press escape to exit from anywhere, not just within the levels.

```
30    while start_game==False:
31        for event in pygame.event.get():
32            if event.type==pygame.KEYDOWN:
33                if event.key==pygame.K_ESCAPE:
34                    game_over=True
35                elif event.key==pygame.K_RETURN or event.key==
                        pygame.K_KP_ENTER:
36                    resume=False
37                    start_game=True
38                elif event.key==pygame.K_LSHIFT or event.key==
                        pygame.K_RSHIFT:
39                    resume=True
40                    start_game=True
41
42    if resume==True: #if they want to pick up a saved game
43        if os.path.exists("savedata.dat")==True:
44            game.load_game()
```

Lines 30 to 40 wait for the user to press a key. The instructions tell them to press Enter to start a new game or Shift to resume an existing one - however because there are two "enter" keys (the one under Backspace and the one alongside the numeric keypad) we have to handle this in line 35. Similarly, there are two shift keys and line 38 captures this and sets the *resume* variable to *True*.

On line 42 we check to see if they chose to continue an existing game but we first need to check if a save file already exists (there won't be one if it's the first time they've played the game) - this is achieved through the *os* ("operating system") module function. On line 44, we run a yet-to-be-created function of the Game object.

```
46    #MAIN GAME LOOP
47    while game.get_level()<=NUMBER_OF_LEVELS and game_over==False:
48
49        #SHOW LEVEL NUMBER
50        surface.fill(BLACK)
51        levelText=displayFont.render('Level: '+str(game.get_level
          ()),True,GREEN)
52        surface.blit(levelText,(150,300))
53        pygame.display.update()
54        pygame.time.wait(1500)
55
56        #SET UP VARIABLES FOR LEVEL
57        game.save_game()
58        live_fruit_sprites=pygame.sprite.Group()
59        game._raspberries_saved=0
60        bullet_sprites=pygame.sprite.Group()
61        other_sprites=pygame.sprite.Group()
62        turret=Turret(WINDOWWIDTH,WINDOWHEIGHT)
63        other_sprites.add(turret)
64        ticktock=1
65        level_over=False
66
67        #PLAY INDIVIDUAL LEVEL
68        while level_over==False and game_over==False:
69            for event in pygame.event.get():
70                if event.type==pygame.KEYDOWN:
71                    if event.key==pygame.K_ESCAPE:
72                        game_over=True
73                    elif event.key==pygame.K_LEFT:
74                        turret.update_position("left",WINDOWWIDTH,
                         game.get_level())
75                    elif event.key==pygame.K_RIGHT:
76                        turret.update_position("right",WINDOWWIDTH,
                         game.get_level())
77                    elif event.key==pygame.K_SPACE:
78                        bullet=Bullet(turret.get_gun_position())
79                        bullet_sprites.add(bullet)
```

The biggest change to the structure of the program is to add a new loop which runs while the current level is less than or equal to the total number of levels and the user hasn't elected to exit by pressing escape. Before each level begins, we want to display a text message so, on lines 50 to 54, we erase the splash screen by filling it with black, set up a font (we've changed the name of this variable from *scoreFont* because it now has a more general use). This is then displayed and we use *pygame's time.wait()* function to pause for 1.5 seconds.

Once the time is up, we start the code for each level (remember, the code after line 47 will run each time a new level is started). On line 57 we run another function of *Game* we haven't yet written to save progress. Why save it now? Because we want the user to come back at the start of the level they were playing when they exited so we preserve the state before they began that level. The only other changes to this block of code are that we zero the variable *game._raspberries_saved* before the level starts and we create a new variable *level_over*.

Most of the code from the main loop of the basic game remains unchanged - except for two major differences. The first is that we've indented the code by exactly one tab (do this in Geany by highlighting every line from *#PLAY INDIVIDUAL LEVEL* down to *clock.tick(FPS)* and pressing tab once to place the whole loop inside the main game loop starting at line 47. If you think this through you'll see why we've done this - for each level we need to run the code that displays the fruit and other sprites and handles collisions etc. At the end of the level we then loop back to line 47 to see if we've reached the final level or not.

You'll see on line 68 that we're testing two conditions - the level will play if *level_over* isn't *True* and if they haven't pressed *escape* to end the game. The event handling code is unchanged but we've simplified the code for adding new fruits to the screen - we're now doing this every time ticktock reaches 120 which, for level 1, will be 4 seconds (30 frames per second into 120).

```
81      if ticktock >=120:
82          ticktock=0
83          if len(live_fruit_sprites)<10:
84              live_fruit_sprites.add((Fruit(WINDOWWIDTH)))
85
86      for sprite in bullet_sprites:
87          sprite.update_position()
88
89      collisions=pygame.sprite.groupcollide(
        live_fruit_sprites,bullet_sprites,False,True)
90
91      if collisions: #if there are any
92          for fruit in collisions: #go through all
            collisions and check
93              fruit.shot(game)
94
95      background=pygame.image.load("images/gameBoard.png")
96      surface.blit(background,(0,0))
97      bullet_sprites.draw(surface)
98      other_sprites.draw(surface)
99
100     for sprite in live_fruit_sprites:
101         sprite.update_position(game.get_level(),
            WINDOWHEIGHT,game)
102     live_fruit_sprites.draw(surface)
103
104     scoreText=displayFont.render('Score: '+str(game.
        get_score()),True,GREEN)
105     levelText=displayFont.render('Level: '+str(game.
        get_level()),True, WHITE)
106     raspberriesText=displayFont.render('Raspberries: '+str(
        game.get_raspberries_saved()),True,RED)
107     surface.blit(scoreText,(10,10))
108     surface.blit(levelText,(10,50))
109     surface.blit(raspberriesText,(10,90))
110     pygame.display.update()
111     ticktock+=game.get_level()
```

On lines 95 and 96 we load a more interesting background - an 8-bit PNG. The code then remains unchanged until line 102 when we add a new parameter to the *update_position* function of the *Fruit* class - we'll come to this when we look at the changes to that class.

Lines 106 to 112 have been enhanced to add extra player information including the current level and the number of raspberries saved so far. On line 117 we call a new function of the *Game* object to increment the level if ten raspberries have reached the bottom of the screen. We then set *level_over* to *True* so that the level exits and Python loops back to line 47.

```
112
113          if game.get_raspberries_saved()>=10:
114              game.update_level(1)
115              level_over=True
116          clock.tick(FPS)
117
118      #handle end of game
119
120      surface.fill(BLACK)
121      scoreText=displayFont.render('Game over. Score: '+str(game.
         get_score()),True,GREEN)
122      surface.blit(scoreText,(10,200))
123      pygame.display.update()
124
125      raw_input("press any key")
126
127  if __name__ == '__main__':
128      main()
129
```

The only change to the last few lines is to add a summary to the final screen showing their overall score.

game.py

```
1   import pickle
2   class Game():
3       def __init__(self):
4           self._score=0
5           self._raspberries_saved=0
6           self._level=1
7
8       def update_score(self,amount):
9           self._score+=amount*self._level
10
11      def get_score(self):
12          return self._score
13
14      def update_raspberries_saved(self):
15          self._raspberries_saved+=1
16
17      def get_raspberries_saved(self):
18          return self._raspberries_saved
19
20      def update_level(self,amount):
21          self._level+=amount
22
23      def get_level(self):
24          return self._level
25
26      def save_game(self):
27          save_data={'score':self._score,'level':self._level}
28          save_file=open("savedata.dat","wb")
29          pickle.dump(save_data,save_file)
30
31      def load_game(self):
32          progress_file=open("savedata.dat","rb")
33          progress_data=pickle.load(progress_file)
34          self._score=progress_data['score']
35          self._level=progress_data['level']
```

The main change to game.py is to add the code for saving and loading the player's progress. So, on line 1 we import the *pickle* module. We've also added functions to update the score - you'll notice that on line 9 we multiply the amount the score changes by the level number so the further through the game they are the bigger the rewards for hitting the right fruit (and the deductions for shooting a raspberry!). We also add functions to update and get the level numbers.

The interesting stuff starts at line 26. The code here is very similar to the examples in the section on Python libraries. On line 27 we create a *dictionary* containing the data we want to save (just score and level numbers for this game but we could include the player's name for example). We then open a file to save the data (if it didn't already exist, Python would create the file) and then "dump" it to save.

The *load_game* function is almost exactly the reverse and we end by loading the data into the object. So, if the user had reached level 3 with a score of 1234 when they pressed escape, on restarting the game, pickle would load that data and game._level would now be 3 and game._score would be 1234, exactly as if they had never exited.

fruit.py

```
1   import pygame, random
2   class Fruit(pygame.sprite.Sprite):
3
4       def __init__(self,WINDOWWIDTH):
5           pygame.sprite.Sprite.__init__(self)
6           self._species=random.choice(["raspberry","strawberry",
               "cherry","pear","banana"])
7           self.image=pygame.image.load("images/"+self._species+".png")
8           self.image=pygame.transform.rotate(self.image,random.randint
               (-35,35))
9           self.rect=self.image.get_rect()
10          self.rect.y=0-self.rect.height
11          self.rect.x=(random.randint(self.rect.width/2,(WINDOWWIDTH-
               self.rect.width)))
12
13      def update_position(self,level,WINDOWHEIGHT,game):
14          if self.rect.y<(WINDOWHEIGHT):
15              self.rect.y+=2+level
16          else:
17              if self._species=="raspberry":
18                  game.update_score(50)
19                  game.update_raspberries_saved()
20              else:
21                  game.update_score(-10)
22
23              self.kill()
24
25      def shot(self,game):
26          if self._species=="raspberry":
27              game.update_score(-50)
28          else:
29              game.update_score(10)
30
31          self.kill()
```

We've made just a couple of minor changes to fruit.py. Line 8 rotates the fruit image by a random value between -35 and 35 degrees, making their appearance a little more interesting. You could add code into *update_position* to have them gently swing as they fell if you want the full effect!

Otherwise, the only change is on line 14 where we replace the *speed* parameter with *level* and then, on line 16, use that to increase the speed as the player progresses through the game.

turret.py

```
1  import pygame
2  class Turret(pygame.sprite.Sprite):
3      def __init__(self,WINDOWWIDTH,WINDOWHEIGHT):
4          pygame.sprite.Sprite.__init__(self)
5          self.image=pygame.image.load("images/turret.png")
6          self.rect = self.image.get_rect()
7          self.rect.x = (WINDOWWIDTH-self.rect.width)/2
8          self.rect.y =WINDOWHEIGHT-self.rect.height
9
10     def update_position(self,direction,WINDOWWIDTH,level):
11         if direction=="left" and self.rect.x>10:
12             self.rect.x-=10+level
13         elif direction=="right" and self.rect.x<(WINDOWWIDTH-10):
14             self.rect.x+=10+level
15
16     def get_gun_position(self):
17         position={}
18         position["x"]=self.rect.x+(self.rect.width/2)
19         position["y"]=self.rect.y-(self.rect.height/2)
20         return position
```

The final change is to add the level number to the amount the turret moves each cycle. This has the effect of speeding it up as the levels get higher - otherwise the player would struggle to get across the screen in time to shoot the fruit.

Run the game and you should find you can play multiple levels and get a final score. It may not be of commercial quality but it's a complete, working game, and strangely addictive!

Raspberry Pi

If you've been typing this in on a Raspberry Pi then you'll know that it performs acceptably. If you're using a more powerful computer to create a game for the Pi, you must check it on the Pi device regularly. Pi Splat could certainly be enhanced with bells and whistles such as sounds, an animated background and explosions, for example, but bear in mind that the Raspberry Pi has limited power so you may have to rein in your ambitions a little. At the time of writing, it's not possible to access the 3D graphics of the Pi from Python reliably but, once that is added, you will be able to include spectacular backgrounds and game graphics with very little impact on performance.

Sharing your game

Once you've polished your masterpiece, you'll want to share it. Exactly how you go about that depends on who your target audience is.

Sharing with Raspberry Pi and Linux Users

Raspberry Pis, and every mainstream Linux distribution, come with Python installed, and the Pi also has pygame as part of its default installation. If you plan to share your game with users of other Linux distributions, then they may need to install pygame.

Zip it up

To share a Python program with other Linux users, you simply compress the files into an archive (on Windows these are called Zip files) and send it. To do that on the Raspberry Pi, right-click on the main folder containing your game and select Compress. You then choose a file name and type for the package. If you're sharing with other Linux users, you can leave the type as .tar.gz but, if you're sending the file to Windows users, change it to .zip.

However, it would be nice if the player could simply double click a file and have the game run, rather than have to launch Python or Geany and load main.py. To do this, we're going to create a separate file containing the instructions to launch and run it. Begin by navigating to the folder containing your main.py file, right click and select "Create New Document/Empty Document". Give it the name "start.sh". Now, right click and select "Open with Geany".

In Geany type:

```
python main.py
```

...and save the file. This is the same line you would type in the terminal to run a Python file, but we now need to tell Linux that it should execute this command when the text file is double clicked.

To do this, open a terminal and type the following:

```
cd Desktop/Pi_Splat
```

"cd" is the Linux command for "change directory" and it has the effect of moving the terminal into the folder containing the game - replace "Desktop/Pi_Splat" with the location of your game if it was different.

Now, in the terminal type:

```
chmod +x start.sh
```

The "chmod" command changes the "mode" of the file - in this case the "+x" indicates that it makes the file executable. So, instead of launching, for example, a text editor, the operating system will run the command. To see this in action, double click start.sh and select Run.

Sharing with Windows users

Windows doesn't come with Python installed as standard so you can't simply zip up your game folder and expect it to work. Fortunately, a tool called *Py2Exe* will bundle Python and all the required libraries, along with your game files, into a single .exe file that a Windows user can simply double click. The process feels convoluted the first time but only needs doing once - the person you're sharing with does not need to do it.

To begin, head over to *www.rpilab.net/links* to find the Py2Exe download link

We now need to delve into the bowels of Windows to make sure it can find Python. To do this, press the *Windows Key* and *Print Screen* button together to bring up the *System* dialog box. Now click *Advanced system settings*, then *Environment Variables*.

Click *Path* in the *System Variables* list and the *Edit* button. Now, simply add the following to the text in this box (making sure the entry before it ends in a semi-colon):

```
c:/Python27;
```

Save these settings and reboot.

Go to *http://www.pygame.org/wiki/Pygame2exe* and copy and paste the text in the grey box on that page into a Geany window. This is a template specifically written for using pygame with py2exe, so, to get it to work for our project, we need to change the following lines:

Line 45 - change filename to "main.py"

Line 48 - Change project name to "PiSplat"

Line 54 - change project version to "0.1"

Line 57 - change license to "GNU General Public License"

Line 65 - change description to "A simple shoot-em-up"

Line 71 - change the *self.extra_datas* list to include "images" so that the game images, which are in a subfolder of that name, will be bundled into the .exe

...and save it as "compile.py"

Open a Windows Command Prompt and navigate to the folder containing your game using the cd command, for example:

```
cd Desktop\pi_splat
```

Now, to compile your .exe file type:

```
python compile.py
```

At the end of the process, you'll find a new subfolder called "dist" containing the files you need to distribute for your game to run. Double click the .exe file and your game should now run. To share this game, all you need to do is zip the "dist" folder and email it.

Part 5

CREATING A MORE COMPLEX GAME

You've now seen how to create a simple space invaders-style game, hopefully you typed the code in for yourself and you can now take it on and improve it.

This next chapter shows how a more complex game is developed. Rather than typing every line, I suggest you download the complete code and follow through as I discuss the most interesting parts of the code.

The code is here: *http://scrib.me/rpis5code*

You can then use it as a template for your own game - you'll be surprised at how much you can reuse. The code snippets are also on the companion page so you can see exactly what I'm talking about during the next chapter.

The snippets can be found at http://scrib.me/fruit_pi

Behind the scenes of a real world game

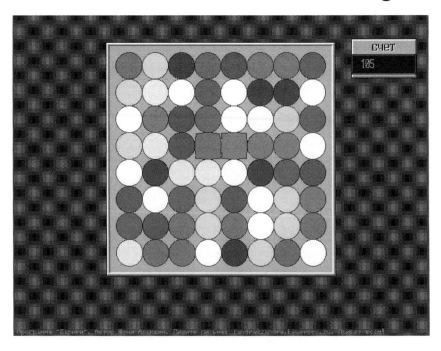

Back in the mid 1990s, Russian programmer Eugene Alemzhin released a game called Shariki in which the player scored points by matching three or more circles of the same colour. These circles then disappeared and the gap was filled by the circles from the rows above with the extra randomly dropping from the top of the board. Sound familiar?

Shariki was the basis of many popular games including the hugely successful Bejeweled series by PopCap Games and current favourite Candy Crush Saga by King.com. Together, this genre has become known as *match three games*.

Fruit-pi is a Raspberry Pi version of this game. Although (in principle) match three games are relatively simple, creating a commercial quality game is a much bigger and more involved task than Pi Splat, our simple shoot 'em up. So, we're going to take a look behind the scenes at the game half way through its development. That way we can discuss the game's design phase, the programming techniques used so far and what remains to be done before it can be released.

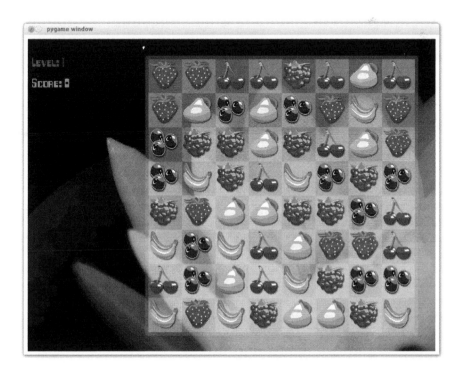

How the game works

As with Pi Splat the first step is to look at the game from the user's point of view – what do they expect from a match three game? Here are the basic rules – these are more or less universal across all games of this type:

- The player sees objects arranged in a grid – usually 8x8

- These objects are pseudo-randomly drawn from a limited selection. In the case of an 8x8 grid, there are usually 6 – this makes sense because too small a selection would result in more of each object and therefore too many matches. Too large a selection would result in too few matches

- The aim is to swap adjacent objects so that, in their new configuration, they form a pattern of three or more identical objects either vertically or horizontally. If no swap is possible, the objects return to their original place

- The initial board for each level should contain no matches (this is why it is pseudo random rather than truly random)

- When a pattern is formed, the objects are then removed from the board and points are awarded

- The objects directly above the space created by this removal then drop into that space. New randomly generated fruits are added from the top of the grid to ensure the whole board is populated

- If this change in configuration causes matches, the game processes them and awards points

- The level is complete when a pre-determined score threshold is reached

Different versions of the game add extra features such as "power-ups" or rewards for matching the same object type more than once in succession

The small number of rules is one of the reasons for the popularity of these casual games – it's not like learning chess. However, translating these simple requirements into a computer program is a different matter. Breaking the rules down into the familiar categories of Input, Logic and Output gives us this initial set of tasks:

Input

The user needs a way to indicate which objects they wish to swap – in the case of a computer-based game, this will usually mean by using a mouse. The final game will also need a way of reading in any saved progress data or stored game preferences.

Logic

The code must:

- Generate pseudo-random sets of objects with no matches for the initial board

- Check for potential matches when the player attempts to swap objects

- Identify which objects to delete as a result

- Generate a new grid configuration that accounts for the removal of matching objects, including the movement of existing objects down the grid and the addition of new objects from the top to replace them

Manage and update game data such as current score and level number

Output

From the player's perspective, games are primary about the graphics, animations and sounds – this is what generates the experience. So the game design and the code written to implement it must include:

- Drawing attractive graphics

- Loading them into appropriate classes

- Animating them onto the screen

- Indicating which fruit has been selected during swapping

- Displaying the score and other game information

- Saving game progress and preference information to a file

- Playing in-game music and sounds

As you can see, that's already quite a list – and each of these tasks can be subdivided, requiring hundreds or even thousands of lines of code. So, even a game you might use to idly pass the time on the bus or in front of the TV represents a big undertaking. Having said that, as we mentioned in part 2 of this book, many of the most successful games have been developed by very small teams – often by individual programmers.

To get a feel for what this means in real-life let's look at how all this translates into the design of a game.

Fruit Pi

You won't be surprised to learn that this game is based on a fruit theme – indeed it uses the fruit graphics from Pi Splat to save time. Rather than shooting fruit, this time we're matching it. As with Pi Splat, the first aim is to get a single level running before then going on to add multiple levels and the various bells and whistles that make for a complete, professional game.

Aside from the fruit images, we need to decide the following:

The size of the playing area: it must be big enough to be enjoyable and easily usable but the bigger the area, the harder it is for low-specification computers such as the Raspberry Pi to keep up. In this case, we decided on a width of 1024 pixels and a height of 768 which is pushing the Pi to its limits whilst still allowing space to make for a good visual experience.

How we will indicate which fruit is selected: the player needs a visual indicator – this might be that the fruit increases in size when clicked or animates, for example. In our case, we opted for a simple rectangle over the selected fruit

How we will animate fruit onto the screen: many games make use of metaphor and in this case this means that we present the fruit as if they've been poured into the top of the computer screen from left to right so we need to reflect this in the animation.

How we will present user information: an 8x8 grid of squares is, itself, going to be square so that means our 1024 x 768 window will leave room for us to display information alongside. In this case we've opted to put the board on the right and the information on the left.

The game background is a single 8 bit .png file and we've also created a separate graphic for the board which is placed on top – this allows us to refresh just that area when the fruits move, saving processing power. The final game will use sounds which we'll source from freesound.org. However, we won't be implementing the sounds until the end of development – we need to get the game mechanics and graphics working well on the Raspberry Pi before we add the extra burden of sound playback. If we didn't do it this way, it would be very hard to know what to optimise.

Programming approach

As with Pi Splat, this program will use object oriented principles – specifically each fruit object will be based on a Fruit class which means it'll remember what type of fruit it is and where it's located on the screen at any moment, along with lots of other information. It'll also be capable of updating its own position and following rules about when to stop moving.

We'll also organise our code into modules. The main module contains the game loop but most of the code related to logic is contained in a logic module and most of the output code will be contained in a module called display.

Under the microscope

Fruit Pi follows a structure that's typical of games and, in particular, games created in Python. The central module, main.py, contains the core of the game – the main loop – with most of the work of generating and displaying the visual objects and handling user interaction undertaken by an array of modules and classes summarised in this diagram:

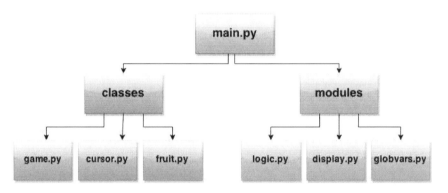

This structure provides good examples of the differences between modules and classes. You can see that each of the classes defines an object that has a clear, individual, identity. The *Fruit* and *Cursor* classes are graphical objects and the *Game* class is used to hold information about the game currently being played – including the score and level.

The modules, on the other hand, are simply blocks of code organised according to their purpose. The file logic.py, for example, doesn't contain a class – it's a set of functions that handle the program's decision making. Similarly, the functions in display.py deal with the visual aspects of the game – including creating and handling the fruit objects. To use a juggling analogy, the class would define the balls and the module would describe how the juggler throws them. We'll see this working in practice as we look at the code itself.

Modules, then, are mainly used to organise code into logical units and they also make it easier to share code across projects. You could dump the entire contents of each module into the main.py file and it would still work – but it'd be ungainly, impossible to reuse and hard to manage.

You'll have noticed that the module names are influenced by our Input, Logic and Output approach (display.py being equivalent to the latter). The only reason there isn't a discrete *input* module is because, for this game, the user input amounts to little more than clicking a pair of fruits so it can be easily handled within the other modules. The way you organise your code must make sense for you (and your team if you're not working alone) and, above all else, whatever approach you use must be practical. If you ever feel a prisoner of the structure you've created, then you've created the wrong structure!

So, from our thoughts on design and by using our Input, Logic, Output approach we can very quickly generate a code structure for our game – we know from the start which objects we're likely to need and which modules to create. We may add or remove classes or modules as we develop but by thinking in those terms we've got a good starting point.

```
1    import pygame
2    ###TOP LEVEL VARIABLES
3    FPS = 30 # frames per second to update the screen
4    WINDOWWIDTH = 1024  # width of the program's window, in pixels
5    WINDOWHEIGHT = 768 # height in pixels
6    BOARDLEFT=300 #the position of the board, from the left
7    BOARDTOP=50 #the position of the board, from the top
8    CELLWIDTHHEIGHT=82 #the width of individual cells
9    CELLIMAGEWIDTH=68 # the width of the image files
10   BOARDWIDTH = 8 # how many columns in the board
11   BOARDHEIGHT = 8 # how many rows in the board
12   NUDGE=(CELLWIDTHHEIGHT-CELLIMAGEWIDTH)/2+4 #because the cell image is smaller than the
13   speed=30
14   WHITE=[255,255,255]; RED=[255,0,0]; GREEN=[0,255,0]; BLUE=[0,0,255]; BLACK=[0,0,0]
15
16   pygame.init()
17   displayFont=pygame.font.Font("256BYTES.TTF",28)
18
19
```

globvars.py

You'll notice one module that doesn't fit this rule – *globvars.py*. As its name suggests, this module contains all the global variables for the game. Now, mention the phrase global variable to programmers of a certain type and they'll throw up their hands in horror because, used inappropriately, they can cause problems. However, it makes sense to use globals for those variables that need to be accessed by all modules and especially where they are constants. We do this by defining them in a separate Python file and then importing it into all modules and classes. Finally, bear in mind that, whilst these are global in scope, they're not defined by the *global* keyword so, from Python's point of view, they're not technically globals at all.

In the case of this game we're defining variables including the height and width of the game window, the position of the game board within that window and the height and width of the cells within the board. We also define some common colours and a typeface.

The Main Loop

Let's look at the structure of a typical main loop for a game – broadly speaking this will be all that main.py contains with all the other work being done by the modules and classes.

```
Import modules and classes

Define variables

Draw the background

Game Loop

    Level Loop
```

So, when the player first launches the game and the background has been drawn, they enter the *game loop*. Unless they've continued a saved game, they'll be at level 1 so the player enters the *level loop* which handles everything that happens within the level – fruit dropping into view, swapping, deleting and so on. Since the *level loop* is inside it, once the level is completed, the player is sent back to the *game loop* which checks to see whether that was the final level and, if not, starts another level loop. This continues until the levels run out or the player exits the game.

Let's take a look at how this works in practice

Imports

We start by importing the various Python libraries we want to use on line 1.

```
1    import pygame, random, time, math, sys, copy
2    from pygame.locals import *
3    from game import *
4    from fruit import *
5    from logic import *
6    from display import *
7    from globvars import *
8    from cursor import *
9
10   game=Game()
11
```

main.py

Pygame is the only one of these that isn't included in a standard Python install – although it is included on the Raspberry Pi. Line 3 to 8 import our custom classes and modules. With these we use a slightly different syntax:

```
from [module/class name] import *
```

The *from* keyword is mainly used to allow us to import part of a module. For example the following line imports just the *randint* function from the Random library:

```
from random import randint
```

This is more efficient as Python is not having to import any unnecessary code but it means that if you want to use another function from the library, you'd have to add it to the from line. By adding an asterisk to the end of the line we import everything, exactly as it we'd used the import keyword, which would seem to defeat the object of using *from*. However, by doing it this way we can refer to the functions within the module by just using their function name rather than having to add the module name also. So, if we use the line:

```
from random import *
```

We can change the following line

```
my_number=random.randint(0,5)
```

... so that it becomes

```
my_number=randint(0,5)
```

In other words, you can treat *randint* as if it were built into the language rather than imported. It saves typing and, in many cases, is just as clear as explicitly naming the module. However, if two functions in two separate modules have identical names then you'll cause an error so it needs handling carefully. One approach is to only use the *from* method of importing with your own classes. This means that *game=game.Game()* becomes *game=Game()* – the first one must indicate which file the class is contained in, the second doesn't because we've used *from*.

This is another reason why you must organise your modules logically. If your code is to be easy to understand, either by yourself or another programmer, you can either prefix all module functions with their name by using import or, if you use the shorter form, have a logical structure to the modules that makes it obvious which one a function belongs to. For example, you could reasonably expect to find a function called *animateFruits* in the display module, you wouldn't expect to see it in logic.py.

Let's look now at the heart of the game – the level loop. This loop runs many times per second and carries out the following instructions during each cycle:

1. If fruits are falling (both at the beginning and when fruit is removed) draw the animation before moving on

2. If not:

   2.a Check whether any keys have been pressed or whether the mouse button has been clicked

   2.b If a fruit has been clicked on

   2.c *If it's the first of a pair*, draw the cursor.

2.d *If it's the second of a pair*, check whether the two fruits are neighbours (if not, they can't possibly match)

2.e *If so*, run the matching algorithm and

2.f *If they do match*, swap the fruits, update the score, delete the fruits, regenerate the board in its new configuration and animate into place

2.g *If they don't*, move the fruits back.

2.h *If the two fruits* were not neighbours, set the second fruit to be the new position for the cursor and await a second click

3. *If no animation is taking place*, refresh the screen

This loop continues to run until a pre-determined score is reached for the level, at which point it exits back to the main game loop. Most of the lines within the level loop call functions from modules or classes which carry out the actual work. For example this line:

```
animateFruits(board,DISPLAYSURFACE,fruit_sprite_group,BO
ARD_AREA,board_graphic)
```

...calls a 34 line function in display.py. By doing it this way, not only can the routine be reused elsewhere in this program, but it also makes it much easier to understand the logic in the level loop. Without knowing the detail of how it works, another programmer could instantly see what the line does. So, main.py is, in a sense, a roadmap showing the primary route the program takes with each module a street atlas providing the detail.

Loading Fruits

Before each level can begin, the game must create a valid board, but how do we represent the board? What sort of variable do we use? Well, remove all the graphical elements and the board is nothing more than a table with eight rows and eight columns and once you're used to Python you'll immediately realise that the humble list is the ideal variable type to store this. If we represent each cell in the bottom row by the name of the fruit it contains then the list for that row could look like this:

```
('strawberry','strawberry','pear','banana','pear','cher
ry','raspberry','raspberry')
```

Which is all very well but we have 8 rows not one, so we make use of the ability of a list to contain other lists – each row, then, is a list of 8 cells. If we wanted, say, to find the value of the second fruit on the bottom row we could do this (remember that all lists are zero-indexed):

```
fruit=board[7][1]
```

In practice, we rarely need to do this, we simply pull the whole row out and then access the row in the normal way.

To assemble the board, the game loop runs this command before each level:

```
loadFruits(board,fruit_sprite_group)
```

As you'd expect, this function is found in display.py

```
16  def loadFruits(board,fruit_sprite_group):
17      cell_number=1
18
19      if len(board)>0:del board[:] #clear the board if there are any fruit objects already there (ie this is level 2+)
20
21  ####### CREATE FRUIT OBJECTS AND LOAD THEM INTO THE LIST BOX
22
23      for row in range(8):#run once for each of the 8 rows
24          thisrow=[] #each row is a separate list
25          y=row*CELLWIDTHHEIGHT+BOARDTOP+NUDGE #set the vertical position for the whole of the row
26
27          for column in range(8):#run once for each of the 8 columns in each row
28              exclude_fruits=[] #list of fruits that musn't be picked because they'd make an immediate match
29
30              if column>1: #check that the two fruits to the left do not match each other (not a prob for the first 2 columns)
31                  if thisrow[column-2]._name==thisrow[column-1]._name: #if the two to the left are the same as this one
32                      exclude_fruits.append(thisrow[column-1]._name)
33
34              if row>1: #now check whether the previous two rows hold the same fruit in this column
35                  if board[row-2][column]._name==board[row-1][column]._name:
36                      exclude_fruits.append(board[row-1][column]._name)
37
38              fruit_name=logic.get_fruit(exclude_fruits) #now get a fruit from the valid choices
39
40              x=column*CELLWIDTHHEIGHT+BOARDLEFT+NUDGE #set the left position of each fruit
41
42              this_fruit=Fruit(fruit_name,x,y,row,column,speed,BOARDWIDTH,BOARDHEIGHT) #create a fruit object
43
44              thisrow.append(this_fruit) # add a reference to the fruit object to the list for this row
45          board.append(thisrow) #add the whole row to the board, as a separate sublist
46
```

display.py

The use of two for..in loops like this is very common when you want to represent two dimensional structures such as a table in code. Line 23 runs eight times, once for each row – during which line 27 runs eight times, once for each cell in the row. Line 25 sets the vertical position of the row, using the global variables to do so – by doing it this way we could replace the existing board with one of a different size by simply changing the values of those global variables.

Remember that one of the rules for the initial board is that it mustn't contain any immediate matches so the *if* statements at lines 30 and 34 check whether a pair of the same fruit already exists to the left of the current cell or immediately above it. If so, then we can't use that fruit for this cell. So, we make a list called *exclude_fruits* of those fruits we mustn't choose this time. We then call the *get_fruit* function in the *logic* module which will send back the name of a randomly generated valid fruit.

```
120  def get_fruit(exclude_list=[]): #however many fruits there are, send back one randomly
121      fruit_names=["banana","blueberry","cherry","pear","raspberry","strawberry"]
122
123      for rottenfruit in exclude_list: #if any of the fruits are invalid
124          if rottenfruit in fruit_names: fruit_names.remove(rottenfruit) #remove them from the list of choices
125
126      fruit_name=randint(0,len(fruit_names)-1) #pick a fruit from the list of valid choices
127      return fruit_names[fruit_name]
```

logic.py

Take a look at the parameters for *get_fruit*. You'll see that we specify *exclude_list* as you'd expect, so that display.py can send a list of fruit names we mustn't choose. However, most of the time, this list will be empty – by setting *exclude_list=[]* we're telling Python that if we're not sent a list, we can assume that there are no fruits and to therefore use an empty list in this function. This is a default setting – it can be very useful if you're not sure which parameters will be passed to a function.

We then create a list with the complete set of fruit names and, in line 123, cycle through the list of excluded fruits, removing them from the list of fruit names in line 124. The if statement in line 124 is needed because if, say, there are two raspberries to the left and two above, then *exclude_list* would contain "raspberry" twice and Python would throw an error if we tried to remove it when it had already been deleted.

Lines 126 and 127 pull a random fruit out of the remaining candidates and send them back.

Once we have that name, we can create a new Fruit object for this cell – we then add this fruit to the row and, once we have a whole row, we add it to the board.

```
this_fruit=Fruit(fruit_name,x,y,row,column,speed,BOARDWIDTH,BOARDHEIGHT)
```

This calls the initialisation routine in the Fruit class and sends it the information it needs in order to create a fruit object. In this case, this means it'll load the correct graphic and set its final position on the board. It also sets a variable called _moving which the code will use later to work out if the fruit is still animating or whether it's arrived in place.

The other functions contained in the Fruit class show how self-aware it is. *calculate_new_position*: works out where the fruit should be the next time it's drawn to the screen. It takes account of whether it's travelling down the screen (as it would be initially), across or up (in the case of a swap) and also works out when to change the _*moving* variable to *False* so that the game can then ignore it during animation. In traditional procedural programming, you'd need to write a complicated nested list to track each fruit from within the level loop – here we leave it to the object itself to do this.

calculate_neighbours: records the fruits above, alongside and below this fruit (where applicable) – this is used later by the level loop when determining whether fruits can be swapped

change_image: when we swap fruits, we're actually changing their image rather than actually swapping objects. This is much simpler and means that each object retains its x and y positions for the entire level, whatever fruit graphic is used. This function handles all the changes necessary when a fruit changes.

Animating Fruits

One particularly distinctive aspect of games such as Bejeweled and Candy Crush Saga is the way the objects – gems, sweets or, in our case, fruit – fall onto the screen. When designing a routine for this, the first step is to write a set of rules for displaying the objects. In this case, the rules are simple enough:

The fruit appears from the top and fills the board from the bottom upwards

Fruit fills from the right hand side of the row.

In other words, when building an empty board, the bottom right hand cell is the first to be filled with fruit and the top left hand cell the last. The implication of this is that we have to build a routine that not only adds fruit from bottom to top but also from right to left.

Remember, at this point we have a list called *board* containing eight sub-lists representing the rows and each containing eight fruit objects, one per cell. Our job now is to animate them onto the screen rather than simply plonking them there in one go (even though that would be much simpler to program!). To make matters more difficult, the row should fill from right to left rather than the whole row appearing at once.

The *animateFruits* function is contained in display.py, as you'd expect, and is called from the level loop whenever the *re_paint* variable is set to *True*. This will be the case at the start of each level as the board fills up and each time fruit is removed by swapping. Here's the line that calls it:

```
animateFruits(board,DISPLAYSURFACE,fruit_sprite_group,BO
ARD_AREA,board_graphic)
```

We send to *animateFruits* the board (the list of fruits organised by row), the pygame surface onto which we're going to draw, the sprite group into which all the fruits will be placed, a global containing a rect of the board area (the x, y, height and width) and a reference to the graphic itself.

The structure of *animateFruits* is similar to that of *loadFruits* in that we're iterating over rows and columns – this time, however, we're altering the position of the fruit each cycle.

```
51  def animateFruits(board,DISPLAYSURFACE,fruit_sprite_group, BOARD_AREA,board_graphic):
52      #global speed
53      ##### SHOW THE ANIMATION OF THE FRUITS FALLING IN STAGGERED FASHION
54      clock=pygame.time.Clock() #create a game clock for limiting the frames per second
55
56
57      falling_fruits=[] #create a copy of the board nested list
58      for fruit_row in range(8):
59          falling_fruits.append(list(board[fruit_row]))
60
61      current_row=0
62
63      for fruit_row in reversed(falling_fruits): #the "reversed" keyword starts at the end of the list and works up
64
65          fruit_sprite_group.add(fruit_row) #add all the fruit objects from this row to the sprite group ready to be displayed
66          n=0
67          for fruit in reversed(fruit_row): ##stagger initial positions
68              fruit._speed=speed
69              fruit._current_y+=n #add n to the starting position of the fruit
70              n-=speed #makes n smaller (negative numbers) so the starting position goes up the screen off the page
71
72          while len(fruit_row)>0: #while there are any fruits still in fruit_row (ie still in motion)
73
74              for fruit in fruit_row: #for each fruit in the row
75                  fruit.move_me() #move it
76                  if fruit._moving==False: # if it's reached the bottom
77                      fruit_row.remove(fruit) #remove it from fruit_row
78
79              shrinking_board_area=(BOARD_AREA[0],BOARD_AREA[1],BOARD_AREA[2],BOARD_AREA[3]-(CELLWIDTHHEIGHT*(current_row-1)))
80
81              DISPLAYSURFACE.blit(board_graphic,shrinking_board_area) #only blit the bit of the board over which the fruits are falling
82
83              fruit_sprite_group.draw(DISPLAYSURFACE) # draw the sprites in their new positions to the surface
84              pygame.display.update(shrinking_board_area) # update only the animated part of the display
85              clock.tick(60)# Limit to 60 fps
86          current_row+=1
```

We begin in lines 58 and 59 of *display.py* by making a copy of the *board* list – we'll see why later. In line 63 we begin the row by row loop – note we use the *reversed* keyword to start at the end of the list (the bottom row) and work upwards. On line 65, we add the entire row to the sprite group and in lines 67 to 70 we work through each fruit (again using *reversed*, this time to work from right to left) moving the vertical position further above the top of the board as we go. In other words, we begin with a staggered line with the left hand fruit much further off-screen than the right.

For each fruit in the row, we then run its *move_me* function which, itself, launches the *calculate_new_position* function we covered earlier. We then check whether the fruit has set its _moving property to *False* – indicating that it's arrived at its final position – and if so we remove the reference to that row from *fruit_row*. This means that we use fewer resources as each fruit stops moving and that we can use the *len* function in line 72 to check when the row has completed. If we'd been using the actual board variable, it'd end up containing no fruits - this is why we copied it.

Line 79 calculates the minimum area that the fruit will pass over as it falls. As the rows build up from the bottom, we don't need to redraw the board behind the settled rows every cycle so this area gets smaller and smaller. We feed this calculation into line 81's *blit* operation which draws the board. We then draw the fruit sprite group in one go but only update the shrinking board area. Whilst the game would work if we drew the whole board each cycle, only redrawing the necessary area is more efficient and will make it more likely a low-specified computer such as the Raspberry Pi can keep up.

The program now waits for the user to click on one of the fruits on the game board. Just as with key presses, pygame offers the ability to listen for mouse events. In this case, the MOUSEBUTTONDOWN event. We need to know which fruit the mouse pointer was over when the button was clicked and this is handled in the *logic.py* function *which_fruit*.

```
120  def get_fruit(exclude_list=[]): #however many fruits there are, send back one randomly
121      fruit_names=["banana","blueberry","cherry","pear","raspberry","strawberry"]
122
123      for rottenfruit in exclude_list: #if any of the fruits are invalid
124          if rottenfruit in fruit_names: fruit_names.remove(rottenfruit) #remove them from the list of choices
125
126      fruit_name=randint(0,len(fruit_names)-1) #pick a fruit from the list of valid choices
127      return fruit_names[fruit_name]
```

Again, we use the loop within a loop approach to access each fruit in each row. We then use a handy pygame sprite function called *collidepoint*. This takes a single parameter, the *event.pos* sent back by the MOUSEBUTTONDOWN event (this is actually two numbers – the x and y positions) and returns *True* if that position is within the bounds of the fruit being examined. So, we go through each fruit waiting for *collidepoint* to be *True* and, when it is, we return the current fruit because we know that this is the one under the mouse pointer.

```
56      if clicked_fruit: #if the mouse has been clicked over a fruit
57          if pair_of_fruits['source']==None:
58              pair_of_fruits['source']=clicked_fruit
59              decoration_sprite_group.add(cursor)
60              cursor.moveMe(clicked_fruit._rect)
61          else:
62              result=check_for_neighbour(pair_of_fruits['source'],clicked_fruit)
63              is_it_a_neighbour=result[0]
64              direction=result[1]
65              if is_it_a_neighbour:
66                  pair_of_fruits['dest']=clicked_fruit
67                  board=swap_fruits(pair_of_fruits,direction,board)
68                  result=handle_matches(board,pair_of_fruits)
69                  if result[0]==True: #if there were matches
70                      pair_of_fruits['source']=None
71                      game.update_score(result[1])
72                      re_paint=True
73                  else:
74                      if direction=="down":
75                          direction="up"
76                      elif direction=="up":
77                          direction="down"
78                      elif direction=="left":
79                          direction="right"
80                      else:
81                          direction="left"
82                      swap_fruits(pair_of_fruits,direction,board)

84                      re_paint=True
85              else:
86                  pair_of_fruits['source']=clicked_fruit
87                  decoration_sprite_group.add(cursor)
88                  cursor.moveMe(clicked_fruit._rect)
```

main.py -clicked_fruit

Back in main.py we now check whether this was the first fruit to be clicked in a pair by establishing whether *pair_of_fruits['source']* already contains a fruit – if not we assume this is the first click, move the cursor over this fruit and wait for the player to click again.

Otherwise, the *else* at line 61 would be triggered and we'd begin by finding out if the second fruit was a neighbour of the first. If it wasn't, then we'd consider this a "new" first click as we imagine that the player has found a match elsewhere. If the second fruit is a neighbour of the first then we must check whether there is a match and, if so, increment the score and update the screen. If not, we swap the fruits back to their original positions and go back to square one.

Finishing the game

So far, the code builds a playing board, animates the pieces into place and handles the player's attempt at matching fruit – but how do we judge whether the match is a valid one? The first step is to check whether the fruits that the player has selected are neighbours. The *check_for_neighbours* function in *logic.py* does this:

```
31  def check_for_neighbour(first_fruit,second_fruit):
32      if second_fruit._row==first_fruit._row and second_fruit._column==first_fruit._neighbours['left']:
33          return (True,'left')
34      elif second_fruit._row==first_fruit._row and second_fruit._column==first_fruit._neighbours['right']:
35          return (True,'right')
36      elif second_fruit._row==first_fruit._neighbours['up'] and second_fruit._column==first_fruit._column:
37          return (True,'up')
38      elif second_fruit._row==first_fruit._neighbours['down'] and second_fruit._column==first_fruit._column:
39          return (True,'down')
40      else:
41          return (False,None)
```

logic.py - check_for_neighbours

Remember that when we created each fruit object we ran a function that established its immediate neighbours. Take a look at line 32 and how this would translate into plain English:

If both fruits are on the same row AND the second fruit's column number is the same as the first fruit's neighbour on the left then they must be neighbours.

We then check the same on the right then, in lines 36 and 38, we work out whether they are neighbours above or below. If any of these returns a True result, we immediately return this, along with the direction. If none is True, we return False because they cannot be neighbours.

Assuming they are neighbours, we must now work out whether, by swapping the fruits into the place the player intends, we'd make a pattern of at least three fruits in a vertical or horizontal line.

```
 4  ⬦⊟def check for matches(board,pair of fruits):
 5         copy_board=copy.deepcopy(board) #we make a copy so that we can work on it without affecting the original
 6
 7         #first check for row matches
 8         any_matches=False #use this to track if there were any matches at all
 9         row=0
10  ⊟    for fruit_row in copy_board:
11            col=0
12  ⊟        for fruit in fruit_row:
13  ⊟            if col<6: #we only need to check the first 6 fruits in the row
14  ⊟                if fruit_row[col+1]._name==fruit_row[col+2]._name==fruit._name:
15                        #are the two fruits to the right the same as this one?
16                        any_matches=True
17                        fruit._delete=True; fruit_row[col+1]._delete=True; fruit_row[col+2]._delete=True
18  ⊟            if row<6: #again, we only need to check the first 6 fruits in a column
19  ⊟                if copy_board[row+1][col]._name==copy_board[row+2][col]._name==fruit._name:
20                        #are the two fruits below the same as this one?
21                        any_matches=True
22                        fruit._delete=True;copy_board[row+1][col]._delete=True;copy_board[row+2][col]._delete=True
23                col+=1
24            row+=1
25
26        return_parameters=[any_matches]
27
28  ⊟    if any_matches==True:
29            return_parameters.append(copy_board)
30
31        return return_parameters
```

Finding matches is pretty straightforward and we begin by making a copy of the board so we can work on it without changing the original. We then use our familiar double *for..in* structure to go through each row and column. Note, on line 13, that we only need to check the first six fruits in a row because any pattern that begins with the seventh would be too short to be valid – the same applies to columns. For each fruit, we check to see whether the two fruits to its right are the same as it. If so, we set the *_delete* property to *True* for all three fruits – this has no effect other than to mark the fruit for deletion later.

We repeat this for the columns from line 18 and send back both the *any_matches* variable (which will be either True or False) and, if True, the copy of the board. This contains copies of all the fruit objects – those that are part of a matching pattern having their *_delete* property set to True.

```
58   def delete_matches(copy_board,board):
59       #now assemble a list of all the fruits that are to be deleted
60       delete_fruits=[]
61       extra_fruits_needed=[0,0,0,0,0,0,0,0]
62       last_affected_row=[0,0,0,0,0,0,0,0]
63
64       row=0
65       for fruit_row in copy_board:
66           column=0
67           for fruit in fruit_row:
68
69               if fruit._delete==True:
70                   extra_fruits_needed[column]+=1
71                   last_affected_row[column]=row
72                   delete_fruits.append(fruit)
73               column+=1
74           row+=1
75
76       #generate the new board
77       row=0
78       col=0
79       for number_of_new_fruits in extra_fruits_needed:
80           if number_of_new_fruits>0:
81               lastrow=last_affected_row[col]
82               for thisrow in range(lastrow,number_of_new_fruits-1,-1):
83                   board[thisrow][col]._current_y=board[thisrow-number_of_new_fruits][col]._y
84                   board[thisrow][col].change_image(board[thisrow-number_of_new_fruits][col]._name,\
85                   board[thisrow-number_of_new_fruits][col]._x,board[thisrow][col]._current_y)
86                   board[thisrow][col]._moving=True
87                   board[thisrow][col]._direction="down"
88
89               y=-80
90               for thisrow in range(0,number_of_new_fruits):
91                   board[thisrow][col]._current_y=y
92                   board[thisrow][col].change_image(get_fruit(),board[thisrow][col]._x,board[thisrow][col]._current_y)
93                   board[thisrow][col]._moving=True
94                   board[thisrow][col]._direction="down"
95                   y-=60
96           col+=1
97
98       number_of_fruits_matches=len(delete_fruits)
99       return (number_of_fruits_matches,board)
```

logic.py - delete_matches

delete_matches is the most important function in the entire program – it both removes the old fruits and generates a new board with all the necessary changes made. We begin by creating two lists, both of eight elements (one for each column of the board). Each element of the first list, *extra_fruits_needed*, represents the number of new fruits that need to be generated for that column. The second list contains the number of the last row that is affected by the changes, again by column. This enables us to simply ignore those rows since they remain the same.

At this point, we need to think about how we're going to handle fruits disappearing and being added. From the player's perspective, they see a gap appearing and fruit dropping to fill the gap. However, this would mean our fruit objects would then be out of sync with their original board locations so a simpler approach would be to simply change the fruit names to match the new board. So, if three raspberries disappear and the next fruit above the gap is a cherry, the player expects to see the cherry drop into the place of the bottom raspberry. In this case, then, we simply change the bottom raspberry to a cherry. The middle raspberry would be changed to match the fruit three rows above it and so on.

On line 79 we begin iterating over *extra_fruits_needed*. In lines 83 to 87 we're swapping the fruits that have disappeared with those above the gap and then, to give the correct visual effect, we change their physical location so that their y position is set to be the same as the fruit whose variety we've stolen. In the above example, the bottom raspberry (which will disappear) is turned into a cherry and moved to the y position of the original cherry – it then animates down to its original position so that it appears that the cherry has dropped into place.

Lines 90 to 94 add the new fruits to the board – but remember we're not creating new fruit objects, we're just giving new fruit names to them. If three fruits are matched vertically, then once the fruits above have dropped into the gap, we'll still need to top up with three more to replace those that have disappeared. So, we generate random names for this column, load in the graphics and set the new fruits above the board out of sight so they can be animated into place.

There's one other situation we must deal with what if the board generated after the player has matched fruit itself has matches? That's easy – once the fruits have animated back into position, we run the *check_for_matches* process again. It doesn't care whether the board it's been sent was created by a user swapping fruits or as a result of being regenerated, it'll check through and report any matches. So, by writing modular code, we're able to reuse the *animate_fruits* and *check_for_matches* procedures to handle both the initial board and the generated board *with no additional work*.

Next Steps

At this stage, we have a fully working single level so the next step is to implement multiple levels, along with a splash screen, instructions and a function to save progress. The graphics and animations will need a little extra polish and sound effects are more or less mandatory. However, before these bells and whistles are added, the fully-working game must be thoroughly tested on the Raspberry Pi.

Fortunately, as this is a puzzle game, performance isn't critical but any additional pizzazz is only going to make performance worse so everything must be done to optimise the basic version for the slower platform before adding anything else. If you intend to release your game for more powerful computers then you can omit this stage but you'd be narrowing your audience. The best approach is to optimise as far as you can and only add the minimum of extra graphical overhead to the final game – that way it should work well on all platforms.

Tips for Programming Games

Visualise what you want to achieve, break it down and get each part fully working before moving on. In the case of this game, the first main visual step is to create the board with all the pieces of fruit in place. So the programming for this was completed first before the animation was then considered and that was completed before the interactive features and judging mechanism was added. By doing it this way, even though it sometimes means rewriting code when you move to the next stage, you always build that stage on a fully working foundation.

1. *Code – Test – Code – Test.* On a similar theme, remember that coding is done in small steps – you write a line or, more often, a short block and you test it. It almost never works first time so you amend your code and test again. Once it's working, you can move on

2. *Write it down!* Don't be afraid to pull out a pen and paper when you get stuck. It can be hard to visualise the effect of what you're doing sometimes but by drawing a rough representation of what the player will see, you can work out the consequences of your code.

3. *Use the terminal.* If you're unsure of how a piece of code works and want to try it out in isolation, type it into the Python interpreter via the terminal and see what happens.

4. *Use the documentation.* Python has extensive and excellent documentation, both at Python.org and on third party sites such as www.stackoverflow.com. Don't struggle, the Python community is very helpful.

5. *Write the documentation.* As you're writing your code, use the # symbol to document it. The code examples in this book do not include extensive documentation because otherwise the book would have been huge – the online samples are heavily commented.

6. *Take a break.* If you find yourself struggling with a particular problem, take a break. It's amazing how often a solution to a

seemingly intractable problem can pop into your head when you've rested

7. *Enjoy yourself.* Give yourself a big pat on the back when you get each part of the game working. There is nothing quite like working hard on a piece of code, getting deeply into it, running it and seeing it work on-screen.

Version 0.2

To see the next version of the game, with sounds and multiple levels, go to *http://scrib.me/rpis5code* and download it.

Part 6

MAKE A CLIMATE MONITOR

Pi in the sky

(You can download the code from here: http://scrib.me/rpis6_code)

As we saw in part 1, the Raspberry Pi has a number of features that make it ideally suited to real world projects. It's cheap, small, rugged and needs only a modest power supply. In this section we're going to discover how to turn a Pi into a climate monitoring station you can use to take measurements of the temperature, air pressure and light levels outside and save them in a form you can then analyse using a spreadsheet program such as Microsoft Excel. We're also going to cover how to connect to Dropbox so that our project can share its results across multiple devices. Finally, we're going to look at how to use a Raspberry Pi without keyboard, monitor or mouse so that you can use your Pi in a wide range of small-scale projects.

The Project Objectives

Every home, school or workplace has its own micro-climate which means that, by taking measurements, you are generating uniquely local data. You can use that data to record seasonal fluctuations, for example, or to learn about how climate readings relate to weather.

Here are five questions you might want to design experiments for:

1. Does higher air pressure correlate with higher temperatures and clear sky?

2. Can a trend in air pressure predict temperature and/or light levels? If so, how far ahead?

3. What is the range of temperatures experienced at your location this year? What is the average? How does that compare with the average at your local MET Office weather station and across the region/country? How does it compare with historical averages?

4. Is there a correlation between light level and temperature on any given day?

5. How does the length of the day vary during the year? Is the speed of lengthening/shortening consistent or does it change with the seasons?

In fact, the list of theories to test is almost endless but we're going to design our experiment with these in mind for now – we can always add extra sensors and code to enhance it later.

Equipment List

Whilst you can hook sensors directly to the Raspberry Pi's GPIO pins (or via a breakout board), we've opted for a system based on USB. This makes the hardware setup dead simple (no soldering required) and it also means you could use a laptop as the host computer if you don't have a Pi.

So, to be able to answer the questions above, we need sensors to read temperature, air pressure and light levels as well as somewhere to house them. We're going to use the Tinkerforge system (tinkerforge.com) which is made up of controllers ("bricks") which plug into the Pi's USB socket and sensors ("bricklets") which connect to the bricks.

This tutorial has been written specifically for these components:

- Raspberry Pi: any version will work perfectly – we used a Model A+

- Case: any case will do

- 4 port unpowered USB hub

- The following equipment from Tinkerforge.com:

- Master Brick + 3 metre USB cable and mounting kit

- https://shop.tinkerforge.com/bricks/master-brick.html

- Temperature Bricklet + cable* + mounting kit** - https://shop.tinkerforge.com/bricklets/temperature-bricklet.html

- Ambient Light Bricklet + cable* + mounting kit** - https://shop.tinkerforge.com/bricklets/ambient-light-bricklet.html

- Barometer Bricklet + cable* + mounting kit** - https://shop.tinkerforge.com/bricklets/barometer-bricklet.html

- Optional: Humidity Bricklet + cable* + mounting kit** - https://shop.tinkerforge.com/bricklets/humidity-bricklet.html

* choose a cable length to suit your specific project – if in doubt, get the largest size

** the mounting kit consists of four small pillars – the sensor is fixed to the pillars with the included bolts and they can then be screwed into a mount of your choice

- Raspberry Pi power supply

- Wireless dongle -We used the TP-Link TL-WN723N in this project

- MicroSD Card – 8GB or more with Raspbian and Geany

- Keyboard, mouse and monitor – for use during development only. When we deploy the project, these will not be needed

- Bird nesting box – yes, really! We're going to use this to house our sensors and, depending on how you want to set it up, the master brick. Drill holes in the front and sides to allow air flow (if the holes are big enough for birds to fit through, use gauze or chicken-wire to prevent this) and paint it white to reflect heat. You also need to drill a hole in the back to feed cables through.

Choosing a location

The Raspberry Pi must be within range of a wifi router unless you're able to connect directly to your wired network. The bird box containing your sensors must be outside in a position where it is not exposed to direct sunlight at any time since this would affect the temperature readings. It should be sited around 4 feet off the ground and positioned so that there's reasonable air flow around it.

 The Pi itself must be protected from the rain. One option is to attach the bird box to the outside of a house, school building or garden shed with the Pi inside. You can try housing the Raspberry Pi in a weatherproof box (do not put it in the bird box) but you would need to think about how you're going to provide it with power.

Step 1: Getting started

Most of our work will be spent using the Raspberry Pi in the normal way, connected to monitor, keyboard and mouse. Once we have everything working, we'll move it to its final position and log into it remotely. Prepare your sensors by connecting the USB cable to the master brick and then connecting the sensors to the brick – do not plug these into the Pi yet (you can get further instructions from Tinkerforge.com). Boot into the desktop.

Step 2: Install Brick Software

We'll now set up the driver that allows the Raspberry Pi to communicate with the Tinkerforge brick - the "Brick Daemon" – and a utility that allows us to see the status and readings from the Brick and sensors – the "Brick Viewer".

1 Brick Daemon

Begin by starting LXTerminal and typing this:

```
sudo apt-get install libusb-1.0-0 libudev0 pm-utils
powermgmt-base
```

This will install the relevant libraries, followed by these lines:

```
wget http://download.tinkerforge.com/tools/brickd/linux/
brickd_linux_latest_armhf.deb

sudo dpkg -i brickd_linux_latest_armhf.deb
```

The first line "gets" the latest version of the brick daemon from the Tinkerforge website. The second extracts and installs the driver.

2 Brick Viewer

Once the Daemon has been installed, return to LXTerminal and type the following

```
cd /home/pi

sudo apt-get install python python-qt4 python-qt4-gl
python-qwt5-qt4 python-opengl python-serial

wget http://download.tinkerforge.com/tools/brickv/linux/
brickv_linux_latest.deb

sudo dpkg -i brickv_linux_latest.deb
```

Once this is done, shut down the Pi, plug the Master Brick into the computer's USB port and start it up again. You can then launch Brick Viewer by typing *brickv* in the LXTerminal window then click the Connect button. After a couple of seconds, the master brick and bricklets will appear. Click the tab for the temperature sensor and you'll see the reading it's reporting.

3 Installer Software

Before we go any further, we can make life easier for ourselves by installing Python's Setup Tools library – this will make installing the Python tools we need very simple.

Open LXTerminal and type the following:

```
wget https://bootstrap.pypa.io/ez_setup.py -O - | sudo
python
```

... that's a letter O, not a zero, by the way. Once this process has completed, we'll have access to a new command, *easy_install*, which will allow us to set up Python tools with a single line.

Coding the basic app

You can download the code for this project from http://scrib.me/rpis5code

We now have a working connection between our sensors and the Raspberry Pi – the next step is to make them programmable through Python. To do this, we need to install the language bindings – a code library that forms a bridge between the bricklets and our application.

Begin by going to http://scrib.me/tinkerbindings and downloading the Python bindings to your Raspberry Pi. Right click the file once it has downloaded and extract the contents to home/pi/tinkerforge

We now need to set up the library so that Python knows where to find it and we can therefore import it into our code. Open a terminal and type the following:

```
cd tinkerforge/source
```

```
sudo python setup.py install
```

The first line moves the terminal into the Tinkerforge folder and the second one uses *setuptools* to set up the libraries. We can now use *import tinkerforge* in any Python code we write.

Structure

We want our code to take periodic readings and then save them in a form we can use. If we intend our code to also process our measurements into charts and tables then we'd probably choose SQLite as the method for saving data because it gives us the option to retrieve the results using sophisticated database queries. However, it's much simpler to use a spreadsheet application such as Microsoft Excel or Google Docs to analyse and graph data. So, at this stage at least, we're going to output our data to .csv (comma separated values) format which can be read by all spreadsheet programs. It's a very simple format and, in our case, means each set of measurements will be on its own row.

Since we want to make repeated measurements, our main structure will be a loop, exactly as in a game, except that the code will loop much more slowly – every 15 minutes in this case. You can, of course, pick a different interval.

Getting Connected

Each Tinkerforge sensor has its own unique ID (UID) which allows you to have more than one of the same sensor connected at once. For example, you might want to measure the temperature both inside and out so you'd have two temperature sensors each with their own ID. The easiest way to find out the UID is to start up the Brick Viewer and click the tab representing each one – you'll see the identifier listed.

Once you have the IDs, create a new file in Geany called main.py and entering the import statements we need:

```
1   import pygame, csv
2
3   HOST="localhost"
4   PORT=4223
5
6   AMBIENT_UID="am9"
7   TEMP_UID="bPb"
8   BARO_UID="bMW"
9
10  from tinkerforge.ip_connection import IPConnection
11  from tinkerforge.bricklet_barometer import Barometer
12  from tinkerforge.bricklet_temperature import Temperature
13  from tinkerforge.bricklet_ambient_light import AmbientLight
```

http://scrib.me/rpi_climate

We'll be using pygame to handle keyboard events and the *csv* module to save our spreadsheet file so we import these in line 1. We then set up a number of variables including the UIDs for each of the sensors. Finally, we import four Tinkerforge libraries - the first is the code needed to establish a connection with the master brick and the remaining lines import the libraries for each of the sensors we're using in this project.

Reading the sensors

main.py (main function)

```
15  def main():
16      ipcon=IPConnection()
17      barometer=Barometer(BARO_UID,ipcon)
18      temp_sensor=Temperature(TEMP_UID, ipcon)
19      light_sensor=AmbientLight(AMBIENT_UID,ipcon)
20
21      ipcon.connect(HOST,PORT) #connect to the master brick
22      pygame.init()
23      clock=pygame.time.Clock()
24
25      end_prog=False
26
27      while end_prog==False:
28          for event in pygame.event.get():
29              if event.type==pygame.KEYDOWN:
30                  if event.key==pygame.K_ESCAPE:
31                      end_prog=True
32
33          air_pressure=barometer.get_air_pressure()/1000
34          temperature=temp_sensor.get_temperature()/100.0
35          light_level=light_sensor.get_illuminance()/10.0
36
37          print('Air pressure: '+str(air_pressure)+' mbar')
38          print('Temperature: '+str(temperature)+'C')
39          print('Illuminance: '+str(light_level)+' Lux')
40
41          pygame.time.wait(2000)
```

http://scrib.me/rpi_climate

For now, we're going to write a loop that senses every 2 seconds because waiting for 15 minutes to see if our code is working is clearly daft. We begin by creating variables based on the *IPConnection* object and then one variable for each sensor. In line 21 we make the connection to the master brick. We then set up a loop that's very similar to those we used for our games – it keeps cycling until we press the escape key.

Lines 33, 34 and 35 read the measurements from the sensors and convert them to the standard form: millibars for air pressure, degrees Celsius for temperature and lux for light.

Finally, we print the values. Give it a go – you should see the current readings appear in the terminal every couple of seconds.

Saving to spreadsheet

Dates and times are difficult for computers to handle. Thanks to the ancient Babylonians, our time measurement system is based on the number 60 (60 seconds in the minute, 60 minutes in the hour) which is not entirely computer friendly. Also, the Earth takes is 365.25 days to orbit the sun so, every four years, we add an extra day. However, the most difficult problem is caused by the fact that different locations have different times – and those times vary throughout the year. In the UK we use GMT in the winter and British Summer Time (BST or GMT+1) in the summer.

For our project, we need a standard and accurate way of recording when measurements were made. For example, we might want to compare the time of sunrise throughout the year but, if we stick to local time, that will seem to "spring forward" by an hour in March and "fall back" in October. The best plan is to use GMT (or its international equivalent UTC) throughout the year and add an extra column to our data that records how many hours to add or deduct from that to get the local time.

Fortunately, Python provides libraries to help with managing time – so we need to add the following lines to the top of the code:

```
from datetime import datetime

import pytz
```

The second of these modules, *pytz*, adds timezone information that makes the job of working out how many hours to add a doddle.

Main.py - get_formatted_time

```
23  def get_formatted_time():
24      GMT=pytz.timezone('Europe/London')
25      utc_time=datetime.now()
26      the_time={}
27      gmt_time=GMT.localize(utc_time)
28      the_time['date']=gmt_time.strftime('%d/%m/%y')
29      the_time['time']=gmt_time.strftime('%H:%M:%S')
30      the_time['zone']=gmt_time.strftime('%z')
31      return the_time
```

http://scrib.me/rpi_climate

We've created a module called *get_formatted_time* which returns the current time formatted the way we want it. We begin by defining a timezone using pytz's built in definitions and calling it *GMT*. We then retrieve the current UTC time using the *now()* method of *datetime* before using *localize* to return the GMT equivalent.

In line 28 we create a date in the format "dd/mm/yy" using the string format conventions common across most programming languages. We do the same for the time in line 29 and, in line 30, we store the current zone offset. In the summer, this will be a 1 because the UK time at that point will be one hour ahead of UTC. We then return these to the calling function in the form of a dictionary with 'date', 'time' and 'zone' entries.

Main.py

```
33  def main():
34      ipcon=IPConnection()
35      barometer=Barometer(BARO_UID,ipcon)
36      temp_sensor=Temperature(TEMP_UID, ipcon)
37      light_sensor=AmbientLight(AMBIENT_UID,ipcon)
38
39      ipcon.connect(HOST,PORT) #connect to the master brick
40      pygame.init()
41      clock=pygame.time.Clock()
42
43      end_prog=False
44
45      while end_prog==False:
46          for event in pygame.event.get():
47              if event.type==pygame.KEYDOWN:
48                  if event.key==pygame.K_ESCAPE:
49                      end_prog=True
50
51          air_pressure=barometer.get_air_pressure()/1000
52          temperature=temp_sensor.get_temperature()/100.0
53          light_level=light_sensor.get_illuminance()/10.0
54
55
56          time_info=get_formatted_time()
57
58          this_row=(time_info['date'],time_info['time'],time_info['zone'],temperature,air_pressure,light_level)
59          save_csv(this_row)
60          pygame.time.wait(2000)
```

http://scrib.me/rpi_climate

Back in the main loop, we've removed the temporary print statements and replaced them with the code at line 56 which calls our new function.

On line 58, we then assemble a new list object which contains the date, time and zone information from *get_formatted_time*. For example:

"27/02/2015,14:14:17,0,6.75,1027,594.3"

Main.py

```
8   AMBIENT_UID="am9"
9   TEMP_UID="bPb"
10  BARO_UID="bMW"
11  OUTPUT_FILE="weather_data.csv"
12
13  from tinkerforge.ip_connection import IPConnection
14  from tinkerforge.bricklet_barometer import Barometer
15  from tinkerforge.bricklet_temperature import Temperature
16  from tinkerforge.bricklet_ambient_light import AmbientLight
17
18  def save_csv(line):
19      csv_file=open(OUTPUT_FILE,'a+')
20      writer=csv.writer(csv_file)
21      writer.writerow(line)
22      csv_file.close()
```

Now, all we to do is save this to a .csv file. In line 11, we've created a new constant *OUTPUT_FILE* which holds the name we're giving to our CSV. Lines 18-21 are all we need to add the current measurement to that file. In line 19 we open the file (if it doesn't already exist, it'll be created). The parameter *a+* tells Python that we want to append this measurement to the end of the file. We then create a new object based on the csv object and, on line 21, we use the csv library's *writerow* function to save the measurements to the .csv file as a single line. We then close the file.

If you run the completed code for this version of the program, you should notice the .csv file being created and lines being added every two seconds. End the program, open the csv in your spreadsheet program and you'll see that several rows have appeared.

Adding a summary

Even once we've changed the sampling period to 15 minutes - by increasing the interval in *pygame.time.wait* to 900000 (900,000 milliseconds) – we'll still be generating a lot of data. For most purposes this is good. If we want to see if there's a correlation between light levels and temperature, for example, having plenty of data to choose from across any particular day is essential.

However, generating almost 100 rows per day makes looking at longer term trends much more difficult. If you wanted to examine the link between air pressure and average temperature over a month or more, it would be much more useful to have the data summarised and organised by date. Fortunately the work involved in saving a second set of data is pretty minimal – all we need to do is total up the day's readings and then save them once per day.

We're going to do this by creating a class called *Today* which we can call from our main module at the appropriate time. This class has three variables (also called properties) to keep running totals of the temperature, air pressure and light levels. Every time measurements are made, we now add a function to tell Today to update its totals. We also check whether the day has finished.

today.py (update)

```
32      def update(self,day,row):
33          newday=False
34
35          if day<>self._day:
36              self._day=day
37              daysummary=self.summarise(row[0])
38              newday=True
39
40          else:
41              self._temp.append(row[3])
42              self._lux.append(row[5])
43              self._pressure.append(row[4])
44              self.pickle_data()
45
46          if newday==True:
47              self.clear_values(day)
48              self._temp.append(row[3])
49              self._lux.append(row[5])
50              self._pressure.append(row[4])
51              return daysummary
52          else:
53              return newday
```

http://scrib.me/rpi_climate

The first thing we have to do in the update function is work out whether the day has ended. This actually pretty simple, all we do is pass the current day number to the function and check whether it equals the one stored by Today. If, for example, we took a reading at 11.50pm on the 21st of July, then *today._day* would have a value of 21 and the value of *day* passed by the main loop would also be 21. 15 minutes later, however, the *day* value in the main loop would have increased to 22 as it would now be the 22nd of July, so when day is compared with *today._day* they would be unequal and we'd set *newday* to True. You can see on line 37 that this triggers the *summarise* function and sends it the final set of measurements.

If it's not a new day, we add the current measurements to the lists and then save them using pickle – otherwise if the program were stopped at any point during the day all the previous measurements would be lost. Then, on line 47, today's variables are cleared ready for the new day to start from scratch and then the latest set of measurements is added to the new lists.

today.py

```
13    def summarise(self,date):
14        self.unpickle_data()
15        maxtemp=max(self._temp)
16        mintemp=min(self._temp)
17        avgtemp=int(sum(self._temp)/len(self._temp)*100)
18        avgtemp=avgtemp/100.00
19        maxpressure=max(self._pressure)
20        minpressure=min(self._pressure)
21        avgpressure=sum(self._pressure)//len(self._pressure)
22        maxlux=max(self._lux)
23        summary=(date,maxtemp,mintemp,avgtemp,maxpressure,minpressure,avgpressure,maxlux)
24        return summary
```

http://scrib.me/rpi_climate

Once we've read the pickle data into the lists, we want our summary to include minimum and maximum temperature for the day, along with average temperature. We do the same with average pressure and also report the maximum light level – we don't report the minimum because that is always zero (at night) or the average for the same reason.

You can see that, because we've stored each set of measurements in a list, we can use Python's built in functions to make finding the maximum and minimum very simple. Once the values have been calculated, we create a new list called *summary* and send it back. We need to insert three lines into our main loop to trigger the update.

```
98            newday=today.update(time_info['date'],this_row)
99
100   if newday<>False:
101       save_summary(newday)
```

today.py

Note that *newday* will either be False if we've simply updated the current day's running totals or it'll be a list if midnight has just passed – in this latter case we then trigger a new function in the main module to save the summary.

```
30  ┌def save_summary(thedata):
31  │     ──▸summary_file="climate_summary"+".csv"
32  │
33  │┌──▸if os.path.exists(summary_file)==False:
34  │ │    ──▸csv_file=open(summary_file,'w')
35  │ │   ──▸writer=csv.writer(csv_file)
36  │ │   ──▸writer.writerow(('Date','MaxTemp','MinTemp','AvgTemp',
        │                        'MaxPressure','MinPressure','AvgPressure','Max Light'))
37  │ │   ──▸writer.writerow(thedata)
38  │└──else:
39  │     ──▸csv_file=open(summary_file,'a+')
40  │    ──▸writer=csv.writer(csv_file)
41  │    ──▸writer.writerow(thedata)
```

main.py

In this case, because there are more values and it's not necessarily obvious what each one represents, we are going to add a header row to the spreadsheet. So, on line 33, we use the *os* module's *path.exists* function to establish whether the .csv file has previously been created (in other words, is this the first time the program has been run?). If no file exists, we write the header row, followed by writing the summary data line. Note that in this case we use the w parameter for opening the file – this is because we are writing a new file rather than appending to an existing one.

If the file does exist, the code in lines 39-41 saves the additional row in exactly the same way as with the 15 minute measurements.

Using third party services

Python is powerful and easy to use but what if the functionality you're after already exists in another service? For example, you might want to allow users of your latest game to be able to post their scores to Facebook (thus attracting potential new players). The social network doesn't give you direct access to their code, naturally, but they have created an Application Programming Interface which allows your programs to talk to theirs. The API specifies the rules for the "conversation" and which "topics" are allowed.

If you wanted to provide your users with a list of books on a specific topic, you could do that by using the Google Books API, or direct them to their nearest bookshop with the Google Places API. You can even embed Netflix's functionality into your app using their API or save files into the cloud using Google Drive, Amazon S3 or, as in our case, Dropbox.

Dropbox is a cloud storage service. Essentially it works by providing a special folder on the Dropbox server accessible only to the user. When you install the "client" software on your computer or mobile devices, the contents of that folder are copied onto it. Dropbox then keeps all devices synchronised as files are added, edited and deleted. So, for example, if you create a new document on your PC and save it to your Dropbox folder, you could then access the same document on your tablet without taking any other action.

As well as client software and a web application for managing your content, Dropbox can also be accessed via its extensive API. Given that there is no official client for the Raspberry Pi, we have no choice but to use the API – however it's almost always the better choice in any case because it means we can handle the transfer of the file with no user intervention. By using the API we also get much more sophisticated access to Dropbox so we can build more complex and useful features into our code.

Dropbox and Python work well together, not least because the Dropbox client is written in Python. As with most APIs, Dropbox includes its own library which makes connecting with its services possible – in much the same way as Tinkerforge's library makes connecting with its sensors possible.

Before you can do anything useful with Dropbox, however, you need to create an account (unless you already have one – a free account is fine). You can then go to *https://www.dropbox.com/developers/apply?cont=/developers/apps* and, once you've agreed to the terms and conditions, click the *create an app* button. This might seem a bit odd but every program that wants to connect to Dropbox needs its own unique id to identify it to the service.

Give your app a name and leave the access setting value set to *folder*. This means that any Dropbox user connecting to your climate measuring app will see a new folder created in their Dropbox account called apps (if one doesn't already exists) and, underneath that, a subfolder with the same name as your app. In our case, we chose to call the app RPi_Lab.

On the general information page for your new app you'll see an *App Key* and *App Secret* – you'll need both of these values for your Python code. Make sure these are kept private as they give the code full access. You're now set up on the Dropbox server.

The final step before we can start integrating your app with Dropbox is to download the Software Development Kit (SDK) – which is analogous to the Tinkerforge bindings. To do this, head over to https://www.dropbox.com/developers/core/sdk on your Pi and click the Python heading under Download SDK.

Once the SDK has been safely downloaded, right click the file and select *Xarchiver* from the context menu. Extract the files to home/pi/dropbox and type the following into the terminal:

```
cd /dropbox/dropbox-python-sdk-2.2.0
```

...bearing in mind that the folder name might be slightly different if the SDK has been updated since publication.

Now type this into the terminal:

```
sudo python setup.py install -f
```

This uses the *easy_install* library we added earlier to install the necessary Dropbox files. We'll now be able to access all the API functionality through a simple *import* statement.

Finishing the climate monitor

You won't be surprised to learn that we must get authorisation from a Dropbox user before connecting to their account so we can upload the data. To handle Dropbox operations, we're going to create a new module called upload.py with two functions: *auth_dropbox* and *save_to_dropbox*.

upload.py (auth_dropbox)

```
2  def auth_dropbox():
3      from dropbox import client, rest, session
4      import pickle,os
5      APP_KEY = '...'
6      APP_SECRET = '...'
7      ACCESS_TYPE = 'app_folder'
8      sess = session.DropboxSession(APP_KEY, APP_SECRET, ACCESS_TYPE)
9
10     #has an access token been saved already?
11     if os.path.exists('config.dat')==False:
12         request_token = sess.obtain_request_token()
13         url = sess.build_authorize_url(request_token)
14
15         # Make the user sign in and authorize this token
16         print "", url
17         print "Please visit this website and press the 'Allow' button, then hit 'Enter' here."
18         raw_input()
19
20         # This will fail if the user didn't visit the above URL and hit 'Allow'
21         access_token = sess.obtain_access_token(request_token)
22         if access_token:
23             save_data={'access_token':access_token.key,'secret_token':access_token.secret}
24             save_file=open('config.dat','wb')
25             pickle.dump(save_data,save_file)
26             print "Success"
```

http://scrib.me/rpi_climate

Authorising Dropbox

Assuming you've installed the Dropbox SDK, you can now import the relevant parts using the from keyword as shown on line 3. We're also going to use the pickle and os standard libraries.

Dropbox works using sessions which, in this case, you can think of as being one-off attempts to use the service. For each session you need to supply the application key, its secret key and the access type (app_folder in almost every case). Dropbox uses these to establish that your application is registered with them and you, as the coder, are connecting legitimately (only you should know the secret key).

Dropbox also needs to know which user's account you want to connect to and that you are authorised to do so. For this it requires an access token and secret token which are different for each user and each session and can only be generated when you're actually running the code. Bear in mind that, as this isn't a publicly distributed app, this user must be either the person who registered the app with Dropbox (you) or one of the five additional accounts you can add on the app details page.

If you don't want the user to have to go through the rigmarole of authorising your app every time they run the program, you need to store these tokens to use again later. Not surprisingly, we'll be using pickle to do this.

The first step is to save the access information into properly named variables and create an object (*sess*) that's an instance of the Dropbox session class. We'll be using this to connect.

On line 11, we use *os.path.exists* to check whether "config.dat" exists – this being the name we've given the file we'll save the tokens in. If it does exist then the program must have been run at least once before and tokens must have been generated already and saved here – in this case we don't need to do anything further at this point.

If the file doesn't exist then we need to get the user's authorisation. Given that this is a program we'll be running ourselves, we can use a fairly basic approach to this – if you were creating a commercial app that connects to Dropbox accounts you'd need to polish it up a bit.

The first step in obtaining authorisation is to create a request token - this identifies us to the Dropbox server. Using this, we create a URL for the user to visit and authorise our access to their Dropbox account. We add a *raw_input()* statement to halt execution until they've done this. If they have, then the access token will be a property of the *sess* object and we can set a variable to its value.

This variable is actually a dictionary containing two tokens – the access token key and the access token secret and we can then use pickle to save them to the config.dat file. Having done this, we'll be able to reuse these tokens in future sessions – if you wanted to connect with a different Dropbox account, simply delete config.dat and the authorisation process will start from scratch next time your run the program.

Saving to Dropbox

Now that we have our access credentials and are linked to a user's account we're ready to save our data to their Dropbox folder on a regular basis.

upload.py (save_to_dropbox)

```
29  def save_to_dropbox(thefile):
30        # Include the Dropbox SDK libraries
31        from dropbox import client, rest, session
32        import pickle,os,sys
33
34        APP_KEY = '                        '
35        APP_SECRET = '                    '
36        ACCESS_TYPE = 'app_folder'
37        try:
38            sess = session.DropboxSession(APP_KEY, APP_SECRET, ACCESS_TYPE)
39            token_file=open('config.dat')
40            token_data=pickle.load(token_file)
41            access_token=token_data['access_token']
42            access_secret=token_data['secret_token']
43            sess.set_token(access_token,access_secret)
44            client = client.DropboxClient(sess)
45            f=open(thefile)
46            response=client.put_file('/'+thefile,f,True)
47            print response['client_mtime']
48        except IOError as e:
49            print "I/O error"
50        except:
51            print "Unexpected error:",sys.exc_info()[0]
```

http://scrib.me/rpi_climate

Python does its best to detect errors in your code before it starts running but what about problems that occur later? In our case, Dropbox relies on a working network connection and if, when it comes to upload the latest data, it can't connect to the internet, Python will simply exit with an error code and your monitoring would stop.

This is a particular problem for projects like this because we're going to be setting up our Raspberry Pi so that it works remotely without keyboard, monitor or mouse. This means that every time we want to reboot it, we'll have to connect to it over the network (if it's working again by that point) and restart the program. If this was hours later, we'd lose a lot of measurements.

Fortunately, Python has a built in mechanism for handling errors using the *try* statement and its best friend *except*. When Python encounters the *try* statement, it knows that if any of the following code produces errors, there's an *except* statement later on that will handle it.

In our case, we're instructing Python to attempt to upload the data (lines 38-47). If there's a problem with the network connect, an *IOError* will be generated and the first *except* block will run – in this case simply printing a message. Any other error prints some information about it to help us diagnose the problem. Crucially, however, in neither case does the program stop. As a rule of thumb, you should always use this technique when conditions you can't control directly (such as an internet connection's availability at any specific moment) would cause the program to crash.

Now let's look at the code in the *try* block. Firstly, we create a new Dropbox session. We then open the config.dat file and use pickle to load in the access token and secret token we saved earlier. We then assign these to the session object, giving it all the information it needs to connect to the correct account.

We're now able to create an object based on Dropbox's core class: *DropboxClient* which takes our session variable as its argument. We now have the Dropbox API at our command. In our case, all we want to do is upload a specific file to a particular folder but you could build the complete functionality into your application if you wanted including, for example, file browsing.

On line 45 we open the file and then pass it to the *put_file* function of the client object:

```
response=client.put_file('/'+thefile,f,True)
```

The first parameter tells Dropbox to upload the file, *f* is a reference to the file itself and the *True* switch ensures that Dropbox overwrites the file in the user's account. If we didn't use this (it's False by default) then Dropbox would create a new file each time.

The *response* variable contains various data about the file once it's been successfully uploaded. On line 47 we simply print it out so we can see, by looking at the interpreter output, that it's working.

The code is now almost complete – all we have to do now is add a few lines to main.py to trigger the Dropbox uploads.

main.py (dropbox)

```
68    pygame.init()
69
70    clock=pygame.time.Clock()
71    pygame.time.set_timer(USEREVENT+1,1800000) #upload every 30 minutes
72    upload.auth_dropbox()
73
74    end_prog=False
75
76    while end_prog==False:
77        for event in pygame.event.get():
78            if event.type==USEREVENT+1:
79                upload.save_to_dropbox(OUTPUT_FILE)
80            if event.type==pygame.KEYDOWN:
81                if event.key==pygame.K_ESCAPE:
82                    end_prog=True
```

http://scrib.me/rpi_climate

Having imported the upload module into *main*, we add a call to the authorisation function in the main loop at line 72.

We've decided to upload the data every 30 minutes (in other words after every second measurement) and this is achieved by adding line 71. This creates a new event which will be triggered every half an hour in line 78 – at which point we run the *save_to_dropbox* function we just created.

Finally, we add a line to the save_summary function of main that causes the daily summary to be uploaded in one go after midnight. The end result is that every 15 minutes measurements are taken and saved to the MicroSD card, every 30 minutes the latest version of this .csv file are uploaded to Dropbox and then, at midnight, we calculate the daily averages, minimums and maximums, add them to the summary .csv file, save this locally and upload it.

Dialling-into your Raspberry Pi

Our weather station is almost ready to deploy in its final position. We're going to set up a remote connection to it so we can access the desktop from another computer – this means we don't have to have monitor, keyboard or mouse connected to the Pi. Before you disconnect, however, we need to know its network ip address – whilst this might change when you reconnect it, more often than not it will be assigned the same address so this is a good place to start.

To find the current ip address type this in LXTerminal:

```
ip a
```

This will cause a lot of information to appear but we're only interested in the final line, beginning *inet* – specifically you need to write down the numbers that follow it. In most cases, the first three sets of numbers will be 192.168.1. so look for these and add the final 1,2 or 3 digit number.

Finally, we need to install the software the Raspberry Pi will run to accept and manage connections. In LXTerminal type the following:

```
sudo apt-get update
```

```
sudo apt-get install tightvncserver
```

Once this has installed, type:

```
vncserver :1
```

You'll be prompted to create a password which will be truncated to 8 characters – this is the password you'll use when your computer connects to the pi. You'll then be asked whether you would like to add a "view only" password but, in most cases, you won't need one.

We now need to set things up so that this server runs automatically when the Raspberry Pi is rebooted in its new location. To do this, launch the File Manager from the Raspbian desktop. Click View and then check the Show Hidden option. You should now see a folder called .config in the Pi folder. Inside this folder, you should see an *autostart* directory (if it's not there click File/Create New/Folder), right click and select Create New/Blank File and name it *tightvnc.desktop*.

Now, right click *tightvnc.desktop* and open it in Geany. You need to add the following text to the file (be careful to include the space before the colon on the fourth line):

```
[Desktop Entry]

Type=Application

Name=TightVNC

Exec=vncserver :1

StartupNotify=false
```

That's the Raspberry Pi all set up. However, before you disconnect it, it's worth checking that you can log in remotely. To do this using a Windows computer, go to www.tightvnc.com/download.php and select the "installer for windows" entry appropriate for your setup. Download the installer and choose the "custom" option and then deselect TightVNC Server since you only need the TightVNC Viewer on your PC. Mac and Linux users can use a built in remote client or the Java version of TightVNC available from the downloads page.

On a PC, we can now test the connection to the Raspberry Pi by launching the TightVNC Viewer and typing the ipaddress of the Pi into the "Remote Host" box, following it with :1 and then click Connect. You'll be prompted for the password you chose when installing TightVNC Server on the Pi and, once that's been entered, you should see a large window appear with a view of the Raspbian desktop. Congratulations, you've connected your computers together!

You can now safely shut down your Raspberry Pi, remove the keyboard, mouse and monitor, and install it in its final location. Once this is done, you should use TightVNC Viewer to connect to the Pi since this will also confirm that it's connected successfully to the internet. If TightVNC Viewer reports that it couldn't make the connection, this is possibly because the IP Address has changed. In that case you can either guess by starting at 192.168.1.2 (or 192.168.0.2 if your network is set up that way) and moving upwards until you connect or you can log into your router and examine the list of connected devices to find the IP Address.

When you're ready to begin monitoring the climate, load your main.py file into Geany and run it. The first set of readings should appear quickly, confirming that the program is working.

What Next?

Once you have your climate monitor in place, you should start receiving updates to your Dropbox folder every 30 minutes (assuming you're using the same update interval as in our example). The update will appear in the form of a .csv file in your application folder. Make a copy and open it in your spreadsheet – you should see your initial readings listed. Remember to also check the following morning that you've also received the summary .csv file. If so, you now know that everything is working as intended.

Calibrate your unit

We talked about siting your climate station so that it gives valid measurements. If you want to be able to compare your readings with national or regional averages then you need to check them against those of your local weather station. To do this, go to the Met Office's observations page at *http://www.metoffice.gov.uk/weather/uk/ observations/* and find the weather station nearest to you. Look at the current value for temperature and compare it with your most recent reading – if they're more than a degree different then you need to look at whether your box is being heated by the sun or cooled by being exposed to the wind. The air pressure reading is less useful as it depends on how far above sea level you are.

The best way to check whether, at any point, your box is being heated by direct sunlight is to wait for a sunny day and, the following day, open up the .csv file and plot the data. You should see a fairly smooth bell-shaped curve as the temperature rises and falls. If you see a big jump in temperature at any point then it might be that the box is warming up too much. In this case either re-site it, shade it or cover it in aluminium foil to reflect the heat away. This is important because otherwise your maximum and average temperatures will be invalid.

Next Steps

Your weather station will generate useful data very quickly although if you're interested in how temperature varies over the seasons, for example, you'll have to wait a little longer before being able to draw conclusions. It makes sense, then, to have short term and longer term objectives so that you can use the measurements sooner rather than later.

Let's say, for example, that you're interested in the relationship between air pressure and temperature. Once you have a week's worth of data, you can plot graphs of both to see how they interrelate. Here's how to generate your chart in LibreOffice/OpenOffice Calc:

1. Make a copy of the .csv file and open it in LibreOffice. Widen any of the columns that look too narrow.

2. Select the date column first, then hold down CTRL and select the AvgTemp and AvgPressure columns – you should now have three selected columns

3. Click Insert/Chart choosing the Points and Lines chart type – click in the Smooth Lines checkbox and now click Finish.

4. You'll notice an immediate problem in the chart – this is caused by the fact that the temperature values are over a much smaller range than those of the air pressure. To fix this, right click over the chart and choose Insert/Delete Axes. Now, under Secondary Axes click next to Y axis – this adds another vertical axis on the right hand side.

5. Right click over the temperature line (in blue, at the bottom) and select Format Data Series. Now, under Align data series to, select Secondary Y axis. You should see the temperature readings now plotted against a much smaller scale.

Part 7

BUILD A ROBOT

The Raspberry Pi makes the perfect robot "brain", not least because its diminutive size makes it easy to slot into all manner of robot "bodies" and its lack of moving parts makes it durable - essential if you're going to send it where no droid has gone before. Unlike your laptop, the Pi is also very easy to directly connect to hardware so it can drive motors or read the values of sensors. Finally, the Pi can be powered by standard household batteries, making it truly mobile - in fact the cheaper Model A+ variant uses even less power than the

Model B+ and Version 2 so it's ideal for use in a robotics project.

In this chapter, we're going to create a roving robot that you can use to learn about robotics or carry out real tasks - all for a fraction of the cost of buying a traditional kit. The first step is to decide what we want our robot to do and there's no better inspiration than NASA's Mars Curiosity Rover.

Because it takes up to 48 minutes for a radio signal to complete the roundtrip between Earth and Mars, NASA uploads a complete sequence of commands in one go and the robot executes those commands 24 minutes later, one after the other and without human involvement. However, the robot also senses its environment so that if it's in danger of colliding with a rock, for example, it will alter its course to avoid it, overriding the instructions from ground control.

We're setting more modest, strictly terrestrial, goals for our Carpet Crawler robot. In our case, mission control will be in the kitchen while our robot trundles around the living room. Just like Curiosity, however, Carpet Crawler will load and execute a series of commands and our modest mechanoid will be able to take photographs of its immediate environment so that its controller (you) can see exactly where it is. Like its illustrious counterpart, it'll also use a pan and tilt mechanism to capture a wide view while stationary. Finally, the carpet crawler will include an infrared sensor so that it can react if anyone, or anything, walks into its field of view.

A platform like this can be used for all sorts of research and educational purposes, apart from cat photography. It can be expanded to incorporate more sensors both to record the environment around the robot and to help it cope with bumping into objects. Follow this tutorial through and you'll have an excellent general purpose educational rover and, you never know, perhaps the start of a career or hobby in robotics.

Build Your Robot

Robotics is a practical subject so we're going to dive right in and get building - I'll deal with the concepts you need to know as we come to them, so let's get started.

Note: you can find a complete parts list, including links to suppliers, at www.rpilab.net/robot. You can choose your own parts, improvise or recycle old bits and pieces - that's part of the fun - but my instructions assume you're using the "official" parts list. You'll also find all the code used in this chapter at that URL, along with extra photos, hi-res wiring charts and video of the robot in action.

You can also find a page with extra photos and other resources here:

http://scrib.me/pi_robot

Warning: This project involves directly connecting your Raspberry Pi to real hardware. We've taken great care to provide detailed instructions on how to do this safely but accept no responsibility if you damage your Pi in the process.

Step 1: Raspberry Pi

To prepare the Raspberry Pi, load up a MicroSD card with the latest version of Raspbian, add a wifi dongle and install Geany (following the instructions in chapter one). Once that's done, set up the Pi to be used "headerless" (without monitor, mouse and keyboard) by following the instructions in the previous chapter. Before you begin to build the robot, check that you can access the Pi using TightVNC.

We're using the Raspberry Pi Camera Module so, when setting up your Pi, be sure to select "Enable Camera" (option 5) on the Raspi-Config screen. You can always relaunch the configuration tool by opening up LXTerminal, typing *sudo raspi-config* and pressing enter.

You'll need a case for your Pi - choose one made from a non-brittle material that includes slots for the GPIO and camera module ribbons (see my recommended choice at www.rpilab.net/robot)

Step 2: Chassis

I chose the popular, and cheap, Magician chassis which includes two powered wheels and a caster built into a framework that has plenty of mounting points for bits and pieces. It should be possible to use most two wheeled chassis with this project or, indeed, to re-purpose an old remote control toy if you're feeling particularly adventurous.

Follow the instructions (or download from http://scrib.me/magicianchassis) that came with the chassis to start construction - halting after step 5 (don't bother with the "speed board holders"). Skip step 6 and, in step 7, add all the spacers except those at the left and right of the curved edge - we'll need to be able to access this area later.

Before you complete construction of the chassis, you need to add some components to the top layer - this is much easier to do before screwing it into place.

Step 3: GPIO and Servos

Use a nut and bolt to secure the bottom part of the Raspberry Pi case to the top layer of the chassis. We're going to use the top of the case to mount the camera and a GPIO breakout board. The Raspberry Pi + models have 40 GPIO (General Purpose Input Output) pins, many of which you can use to send or receive digital pulses in the form of a 5 volt signal.

Misuse of the GPIO pins is the most likely cause of damage to your Pi, so, to make misconnections much less likely, we're going to use a breakout board which sits on top of the case and connects to the GPIO pins via a ribbon cable. My favourite board uses "paddle" connectors so you push wires into them and push down the paddles to engage - this forms a nice, secure, connection that can be easily released if you want. You can find this board here: http://scrib.me/paddle_breakout. The board comes with four mounting holes, but I suggest only using three leaving out the one immediately above the slot for the camera module - this gives room for the module's ribbon cable. *NOTE:* if you have a Model A+, Model B+ or Version 2 Pi then you'll need a *Downgrade GPIO Ribbon Cable* (see the parts list) to enable you to plug into the paddle board.

Place the board on top of the Pi case and mark where the three mounting holes are, then drill through the marks using a 3mm (or similar) metal drill bit. Now you can mount the board on brass or plastic spacers.

We're going to mount the camera on the Dagu Pan & Tilt kit so that we can move it independently of the robot chassis. This kit contains two identical servos (a specialised form of motor), one of which will be mounted on your Pi case. To do this, you can either use your imagination or, as I did, carefully remove the bottom of one of the servos and drill two 3mm holes, a centimetre or so apart. Pass the nuts that were intended for the battery holder (as they have flat heads) through the holes and into two of the small brass spacers included as "spare parts" with the robot chassis. Position the servo alongside the GPIO Breakout Board and mark where the spacers rest on the case - drill 3mm holes in those positions but don't mount the servo at this point. Plug in the ribbon cable to the GPIO pins (with the central ridge facing the outer edge) and draw it through the slot on the edge of the case before connecting to the breakout board.

Step 4: Motor Driver

The GPIO pins can only supply a very small amount of current - not nearly enough to drive the robot's two motors so we must find a way that allows the GPIOs to switch power on and off but actually supplies this power from a separate source. Whilst it's perfectly possible to build a little circuit to handle this, it's much more convenient, and safer, to use a pre-built module. The chip at the heart of this package is the L298N and the modules built around it come in various forms - we're using the most commonly seen one as detailed in the parts list.

The motor driver works by allowing the GPIO to indicate when each motor is enabled and whether it should be turned forward or reverse. For now, simply mount the module on the top layer of the robot chassis in front of the Pi case.

You can now attach the top layer to the rest of the robot chassis, pulling through the wires from the motors so that they come out next to the blue screw terminals on each side. Finally, take the breadboard, peel off the sticky backing and mount it next to the motor driver module. Your setup should look like the photo at this stage.

Breadboards

Breadboards allow you to connect components together without needing to use a soldering iron. They come in many sizes (we're using a "half-size" version) but they're all essentially a matrix of holes containing spring mechanisms so that they grip cables and component legs that are pushed into them, thus connecting them together electrically.

Take a look at the diagram overleaf - it shows a closeup of one corner of a standard breadboard. At the top, you can see two rows in red and blue (the actual breadboard shows just the blue and red lines). Plugging a battery's +ve terminal anywhere along a row supplies voltage to the entire row - it's usually called a "power rail" when this is done. Plugging the -ve terminal into the other row creates a "ground rail" along the entire length.

To understand how the rest of the breadboard works, look at the circuit. You can see that voltage runs from the red horizontal rail through the orange cable and into the first hole in row 27, moving in the direction indicated by the arrows. In contrast to the rails at the top, in this case voltage flows down the row so it passes into and through the LED, out the other leg, along row 26 and into the resistor then across the resistor and up row 24 into the ground rail. So, whereas the rails are connected horizontally (when seen from this angle), the rows are only connected vertically - in other words, there is no connection between rows 27 and 26 unless you create one (by using an LED in this case).

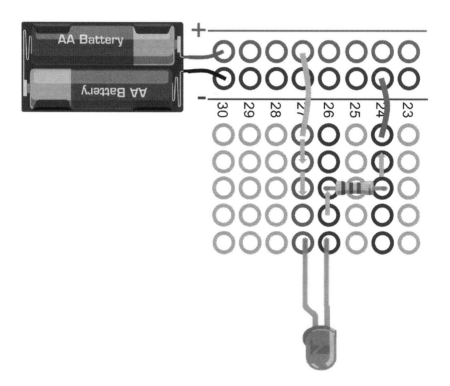

Most breadboards are split into at least two independent regions. In the case of the half size breadboard in this project, there's a valley running up the centre that creates, essentially, two separate breadboards with their own rails and rows. We're using one side for the motors and the other for the Pi.

Step 5: Power

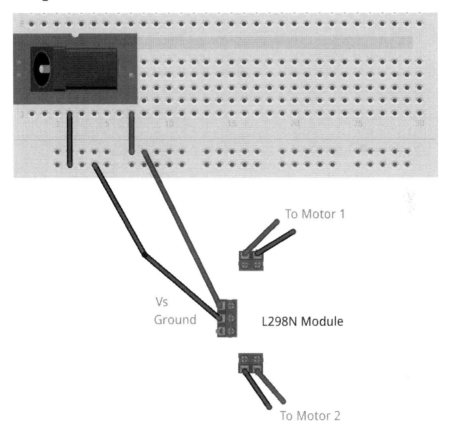

Vs

Ground

To Motor 1

L298N Module

To Motor 2

The Magician Chassis comes with a battery pack that takes 4 AA batteries and supplies power via a barrel jack. In our configuration, we're going to situate this at the front (curved) end of the chassis. Use good quality batteries, ideally top grade alkaline rechargeables providing around 2500mAh as motors consume a lot of current and we're using those batteries to power both the wheels and the pan and tilt servos which also use the 6 volts our battery pack will supply (4 x 1.5v). I used a breadboard barrel jack connector which allows me to send the voltage to the power rail and -ve to the ground rail; this makes for a solid connection but you could simply strip the wire from the battery pack and connect it directly to the rails.

If you're using the barrel jack connector, place it on the breadboard facing the front of the robot. The connector has three legs but the one to the side is purely there to give extra stability - the back leg is connected to the battery voltage and the one nearer the front is ground so you need to use a small patch wire to connect the breadboard row of each to the correct rail. You then need to run a cable from the power rail to the left hand of the three screw terminals on the motor driver (as seen from the front) and a separate cable from the ground rail to the middle terminal.

We now need to connect the motors to the Motor Driver Module. You'll see two sets of blue double terminals, one on each site. Connect the black lead of the right hand motor (as seen from behind) to the top terminal on the left hand block (the one nearest the heat sink), the red lead to the bottom one. Now connect the black lead of the left hand motor to the bottom of the right hand terminal block and the red lead into the final one (nearest the heat sink on the other side). Check the diagram to see how it should all look - you can see that power goes from the battery into the Motor Module and out again through the two terminals to the wheels. If you've got it right, an LED should come on when you make the final connection.

You also need to separately power the Raspberry Pi which requires 5v. You can do this in several ways but the simplest is to use a mobile phone battery pack such as the PowerGen 8400mAh which will keep your Pi going all day. You can also use standard batteries, but since there's no combination of 1.5v cells that equals exactly 5v, you'll need to add a converter. In that case, the best compromise between weight, power and price is a high capacity 9v PP3 battery connected to the Pi via a USB convertor (see the parts list) which steps down the voltage to a safe level. Bear in mind, however, that you'll only get a few hours continuous use out of even the best 9v battery. The power supply for the Pi can sit beneath it on the bottom layer - the PowerGen 8400mAh fits perfectly - and can be connected to the computer via a short micro usb cable.

Step 6: Getting ready to move

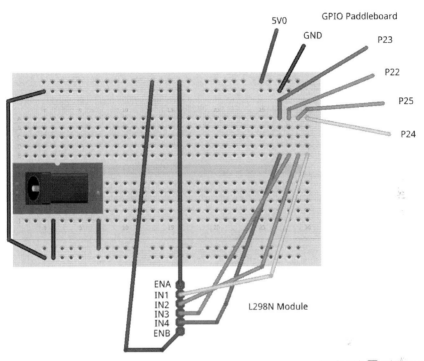

Made with ⬛ Fritzing.org

We need one GPIO pin to control each of the four directions (left-forward, left-reverse, right-forward, right-reverse) so begin by pushing a piece of patch wire into the holes marked P22,P23,P24,P25 on the paddle board, making sure they're nice and secure. The other end of the wire should go into consecutive rows on the breadboard, starting right next to where it meets the Pi's case - this might be rows 1,2,3 and 4 or 30,29,28 and 27 depending on which way round you have your board. Look at the Motor Module and you'll see a row of pins, put a lead into each of them and then connect them to the breadboard so that IN1 is in the same row as P24 - this connects them electrically. IN2 should be connected to P25, IN3 to P22 and IN4 to P23.

There's also a pin on each end - if they're covered by a black jumper, remove it. These pins are labelled ENA and ENB and they turn each motor on and off. Use a female to male lead to connect both ENA and

ENB to the same row on the breadboard (we want both motors to run at the same speed). Now, push one end of a cable into the paddle board hole labelled MOSI (this is GPIO10) and the other into the breadboard row containing the ENA and ENB leads.

Connect a wire from any of the paddle board ports labelled "5V0" to the top red power rail.

IMPORTANT: do NOT connect this wire to the same power rail as the battery!

Now, run a wire from any of the "GND" holes on the paddle board to the blue ground rail at the top and, finally, run one more cable to connect the ground rail of the Pi to the ground rail of the battery. Your wiring should look like the diagram at http://scrib.me/pi_robot - note that I've left out most of the wiring from the previous step to avoid it becoming confusing.

Step 7: Get moving

You can find the code for each step at *www.rpilab.net/code*. Download the code for the first step to a folder on your Pi's desktop called Robot. You can now use TightVNC to access the Pi. You'll need to run the program from the command line in LXTerminal because controlling the GPIO pins requires administrative privileges so type the following (assuming you've just started your session):

```
cd Desktop/Robot

sudo python main.py
```

Your robot should now move forwards, backwards, left and right and you should see messages appearing in the terminal window as it runs through each manoeuvre.

Controlling the GPIO is pretty simple using the RPi.GPIO library. Essentially, each of the pins we plan to use is set up to be used either for input (to read from a sensor, for example) or, as in this case, as output to control motors. Once this is done, we send a HIGH value to the pin to send voltage or a LOW value to turn it off. For example, to move forward, the pins connected to IN1 and IN3 are both set to high.

To go backwards, IN2 and IN4 are set high. To go left, IN1 is set high and IN4 high so that the left and right wheels rotate in opposite directions - this causes the robot to spin on the spot.

To control speed, we use a technique called Pulse Width Modulation which, essentially, involves turning the motors on and off many times a second. In the example code, at lines 51 and 52 we set up the PWM and, once done, the Pi will pulse the ENA and ENB ports as we've specified. You'll see that I've written a function that wraps all this up so we can send simple commands such as go("forward",2,6) to tell the robot to go forward for two seconds at full speed.

Step 8: Snap happy

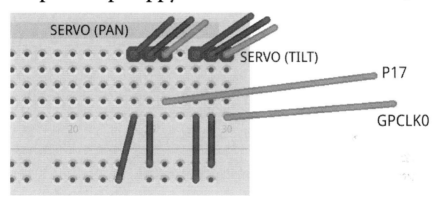

http://scrib.me/pi_robot

To add photo taking capabilities we must first install the camera module and then mount it on the pan and tilt unit. Follow its instructions to insert the camera's ribbon cable into the appropriate connector on the Pi and pass it through the slot beneath the GPIO Breakout Board.

You can capture photos from within LXTerminal using the raspistill utility but Sean Ashton's PiCam library makes it much simpler to do this from within Python. Start by booting up your Raspberry Pi (with camera attached) and typing the following in an LXTerminal window:

```
sudo apt-get install python-imaging
```

This downloads the libraries that PiCam uses to function. To install PiCam itself, start up a browser on the Pi, go to *https://github.com/ashtons/picam* and click the Download ZIP button. Open up the file explorer in Raspbian and navigate to the */home/pi/* folder where you should see the zip file. Right click it and select "Xarchiver" then extract the zip file to the */home/pi folder*. Back at LXTerminal, type *cd /pi/picam-master* and press return, then install the library by typing:

```
sudo python setup.py install
```

It's now time to build the pan and tilt mechanism, making sure that the servo you've mounted the two spacers on ends up at the bottom. Once done, you can screw the pan and tilt assembly to the Pi's case using the two holes you drilled earlier, and then mount the camera module on it using plastic screws. Each servo has three leads that terminate in a female header so you'll need to put six header pins into the breadboard (each on a separate row) on the side nearest the Motor Driver modules, into which you can plug the servo leads - you could also use stripped cable or, if you prefer, remove the servo connectors and plug in the bare wires. Now use small cable jumpers to connect the rows containing the red cables to the battery power rail and also to connect the rows containing the dark brown cables to the battery ground rail.

The third lead is orange and this is the "signal" cable - it tells the servo which position to move to. Take another cable and connect, via the breadboard, the orange lead of the bottom servo (the one responsible for panning the camera) to the hole labelled P17 on the paddle board. The orange lead of the top servo (tilt) should be linked to the hole labelled GPCLK0. That's it, your servos are now connected.

We're going to use the *ServoBlaster* library created by Richard Hirst to control the pan and tilt. To install it, type the following commands into LXTerminal, pressing Enter between each:

```
sudo apt-get update
```

```
sudo apt-get install git
```

```
git clone https://github.com/richardghirst/PiBits.git

cd PiBits/ServoBlaster/user

make servod

sudo chmod 777 servod
```

ServoBlaster allows us to use any number between 50 and 250 to control how far each servo will turn - with most having a total range of around 180 degrees. To simplify matters when it comes to controlling our robot, we want to use commands like "right", "left", "up" and "down" rather than numbers so the first thing to do is to work out which values correspond to which positions. To do this, I've written a program called servotest.py which you can download from www.rpilab.net/code . Download it to the same folder as your main.py and use this command (assuming your LXTerminal is still in this folder) to run it:

```
sudo python servo_test.py
```

You'll be invited to enter values in pairs separated by a space with the tilt first. So, typing 180 120 would set the tilt servo to 180 and the pan to 120. Each setup is different because it depends on what position the servos were at when you assembled the pan and tilt mechanism. I suggest beginning with those values as they'll probably result in the pan/tilt facing front and roughly flat - this is your default position. Lower values will make the tilt move upwards and the pan move left so, by experimenting, you can establish the values to use for left, front and right (for the pan direction) and up, flat and down for tilt. Important: find the central position (front,flat) first using safe values such as 180 120 then add or subtract in tens from there to read the extremes - don't start low or high as it could strain the servos. If you hear the servos whine, change the values. To end the program, type "stop".

You can now download the updated main.py for step 8 from www.rpilab.net/code to replace the code from the previous steps. You should also download Servo.py which is a class containing most of the code for using the pan and tilt - open it in Geany and change the values in lines 5 and 6 to those for your setup. Save and close the file. In the new main.py file, on line 88 you'll see the self explanatory command *servo.move_servo("pan","left")*

I've also added a function for taking a photo - all you need to do to trigger this is to call the function: take_photo() as on line 90. Take a look at all the code from lines 86 to to 103 and you'll see it's a complete sequence for moving, positioning the camera, and taking photos. The only thing you need to do before running the code is to create a subfolder in the Robot directory called "Photos". You can now use sudo python main.py to watch the robot go through its paces. If you're using TightVNC you'll see the photos appear in that folder as they're taken.

Step 9: Sensing Movement

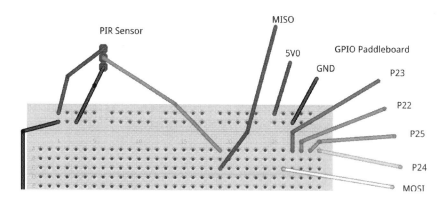

http://scrib.me/pi_robot

Our robot can now be programmed to move, position its camera and take a photo. It can't, as yet, respond to its surroundings. So, we're going to add a Passive Infrared Sensor (exactly like those found in burglar alarm systems) that will be triggered when something warm moves in front of it. The sensor listed on www.rpilab.net/robot is very cheap and easy to use - you can mount it on the front of your robot with a little Blutack.

There are three pins on the top - the Vcc pin connects directly to the power rail from the Pi (it uses 5 volts so don't plug it into the motor's power rail) and the GND pin should be connected to the Pi's ground rail. Whenever the sensor detects movement, it outputs voltage on the middle pin so connect that to a spare row on your breadboard. Run a cable from the same row to the hole marked MISO on the GPIO paddle board. You can now download main.py for Step 9 to overwrite your existing file (Servo.py is unchanged). On line 9, you'll see that we set the PIR_pin as GPIO 9 (this is the MISO pin) and on line 19 we set up the pin for input. The function at line 85 cycles through a while loop in case the PIR module had already been triggered - it continues cycling until the PIR stops sending voltage. It's now ready to wait for movement and, as soon as it's triggered, the function exits. The result is that the robot will halt execution of the script until something moves in front of it. All you need to do is add the function call as shown at line 108: PIR().

Run the script as before and your robot will move forward then pan and tilt. It'll then wait for movement and, as soon as it's detected, it'll take a photo and then go through another sequence of moves.

Step 10: Next Steps

Our robot can now lay in wait for passing pets, or human intruders, and take a picture of the offenders. You can edit the main.py file to create any sequence of commands you like - it's easy enough to work out what the parameters are by looking at the functions themselves. For the final version of my robot, I added a buzzer which sounds when photos are taken or movement detected, along with an LED for giving visual feedback.

I'm using a piezo buzzer because I can then make it sound simply by passing voltage through it - the sound it makes is similar to the startup beeps of a desktop computer. Buzzers are also very cheap and have only two connections - a positive and ground. To make things a little more exciting, I'm also adding an LED - you can either buy one for pennies or "liberate" one from an unloved toy or electronic device. To make it work, all you need to do is connect the positive terminal of the buzzer to a GPIO port (I'm using the one marked CE0 which is

GPIO 8) on the breadboard. Naturally, the other terminal needs to connect to the Ground rail but rather than doing so with a bit of wire, if you drop the longer leg of the LED into the same row on the breadboard as the negative terminal of the buzzer and the shorter leg into the ground rail, you complete the circuit through the LED. So, when we turn on the GPIO port using Python, electricity flows through the buzzer (making a noise), then through the LED (making it light) before reaching ground. In other words, by using one Python command, we can control both the buzzer and the light.

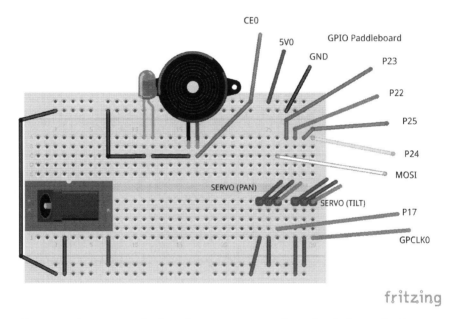

Once you've set up the hardware, you can download the code for step 9. Adding this auditory and visual feedback is very simple. On lines 16 and 31, we set up the GPIO ports we're going to use. We then create a new function from line 61 to make the buzzer beep - it does this by turning on the power for 0.1 seconds then off for 0.2. The function accepts a parameter called "repeat" so that we can make it beep a specific number of times for each purpose. It might beep three times when it first boots up, for example, and once when taking a photo.

I also wrote code to read in an external text file containing the robot's commands so that they could be edited and uploaded in a text editor rather than having to directly alter the Python code as we've been doing to this point. To do this, I created a text file called commands.txt and invented my own simple language for instructing the robot. Direction is controlled by the forward, backward, left, right commands each of which has a for parameter (which is the number of seconds the robot must move for) and a speed parameter - you'll remember that these are the parameters used in the go function in our code so we won't need to change that at all.

We also have a pan command for controlling the horizontal direction of the camera using the parameters right, left, and front as well as a tilt command for the vertical direction which uses up, down and flat. The camera is controlled with snap and the wait PIR command causes the robot to pause until the infrared sensor is tripped.

So, in the text file, you can type a sequence of commands like this:

```
forward  for:2.5 speed:6

left for:1 speed:6

wait PIR

pan front

tilt flat

snap
```

...which would make the robot move forward, then left before waiting for the PIR to be triggered. It would then move the camera to front and centre before taking a photo. The beauty of this approach is that you can now easily get the computer to carry out a complete sequence without having to go into your Python code at all.

All we have to do now is read in the text file, extract the commands and, for each, run the correct function. The code for this begins at line 128 and uses the with and for structures to loop through the contents of the file until it's finished. The series of if statements then works out what command is on the current line, extracts any parameters, and runs the appropriate function. The code has been heavily documented so you can work out what each line does.

As well as making it possible for a non-coder to control the robot by typing simple commands into a text file, this approach also makes it easy to add new functionality to the robot by writing the Python code and adding a simple text command to control it. In fact, as your robot gets more sophisticated, you might want to make your code more object oriented as we did with the games earlier in the book. Whatever you do, have fun - robotics is one of the most interesting areas of computing and there's a particular thrill in watching your creation navigate its way around your home or office performing the actions you've programmed or reacting to its environment. Robots may appear to be science fiction but they're becoming progressively more mainstream and will be used in many aspects of everyday and commercial life. The Raspberry Pi makes it possible to experiment in robotics and create real-world projects for a minimal cost and who knows, today's Pi owner may create tomorrow's planetary rover.

Robots come in many forms

In this chapter, we've built and programmed a roving explorer but many of the robots in day to day use never move anywhere. Robot arms are commonly used in assembly lines and laboratories across the world and, whilst the real thing is very expensive, it's possible to build your own robot arm and control it with your Raspberry Pi at a very low cost. Maplin (*http://www.maplin.co.uk/p/robotic-arm-kit-with-usb-pc-interface-a37jn*) stock a small, self-assembly robot arm which is intended to be used with a Windows PC but by connecting it to a Raspberry Pi we can directly program it to carry out tasks. You can usually get one of these robot arms on ebay (search for "Maplin robot arm") for half the retail price of around £40 – just make sure the one you buy is sealed in its box.

Begin by following the instructions to build the arm and test that it works using a Windows PC and the software that comes with it. Connect it to your Raspberry Pi via a powered USB hub and boot into the desktop. We need to install a few bits of software so execute these commands in sequence in LXTerminal:

```
sudo apt-get install python-pip

sudo pip install pyusb
```

This installs the USB library that allows us to control the robot arm using the Python programming language.

You can download some sample code we've created from *www.rpi-net/code/robotarm* to give you a head start. You can then open them in Geany - feel free to edit *armtest.py* but don't change *Robot_Arm.py* unless you know what you're doing. To run the script, double click LXTerminal and, assuming you've copied the Python files to a folder called "robotarm" on the desktop, type: *sudo python Desktop/robotarm/armtest.py*.

The *armtest.py* file contains a sample routine that moves every joint in the robot – it should be easy enough to see how it moves the arm so try to work out how to get it to go through a set of movements and then return to its original position. Maybe you could get it to stir your tea!

Congratulations!

I've now touched on the main aspects of Python and how it can be used to create software that can be used for everything from games programming to building Dropbox functionality into our app. Having made it this far, you've already acquired the vast majority of the skills you'll need for any career in programming – from now on it's a matter of broadening your knowledge in those areas that interest you and then adding the secret ingredient: practice.

Python can be used for powering websites, creating mobile apps and programming embedded devices – in fact there are very few aspects of programming closed to Python developers. The Raspberry Pi is the perfect companion for Python and I'm sure you've thought of how you can combine the two in all sorts of wonderful and weird ways. In fact, you might find the range of possibilities overwhelming – where should you begin?

My advice is to focus on an achievable project that interests you and then find out if anyone in the marvellous Raspberry Pi community has created something similar. Build something personal to you that makes a real difference to your day to day life – perhaps a Pi-powered door entry system; a heat sensing robot or a time-lapse photography setup. Or, for a start, how about building on the games we've provided – each makes a good starting point.

Being a good programmer is not about memorising the names of commands and functions. It's not necessarily about late nights slumped over a laptop tracking down a particularly naughty bug. It's not the preserve of geniuses who dream code and it's certainly not a purely male preserve. Programming is for everyone. It's about doing something you love – it's the ultimate creative pursuit.

Go out there and make something fabulous – and don't forget to tell me all about it.

You can find the code and resources used in this book here: *www.rpilab.net*

There's also a Facebook page at *www.facebook.com/rpilab*

...but a better choice would be to follow the Google+ page at *www.google.com/+RpilabNet*

You can also follow me on Twitter at *@kevpartner*

19323314R00123

Printed in Great Britain
by Amazon